C000162359

1 MONTH OF
FREE
READING

at

www.ForgottenBooks.com

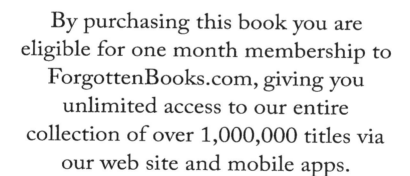

By purchasing this book you are eligible for one month membership to ForgottenBooks.com, giving you unlimited access to our entire collection of over 1,000,000 titles via our web site and mobile apps.

To claim your free month visit:

www.forgottenbooks.com/free897359

* Offer is valid for 45 days from date of purchase. Terms and conditions apply.

ISBN 978-0-265-84032-0
PIBN 10897359

This book is a reproduction of an important historical work. Forgotten Books uses state-of-the-art technology to digitally reconstruct the work, preserving the original format whilst repairing imperfections present in the aged copy. In rare cases, an imperfection in the original, such as a blemish or missing page, may be replicated in our edition. We do, however, repair the vast majority of imperfections successfully; any imperfections that remain are intentionally left to preserve the state of such historical works.

Forgotten Books is a registered trademark of FB &c Ltd.
Copyright © 2018 FB &c Ltd.
FB &c Ltd, Dalton House, 60 Windsor Avenue, London, SW19 2RR.
Company number 08720141. Registered in England and Wales.

For support please visit www.forgottenbooks.com

119.8

PO1
1935

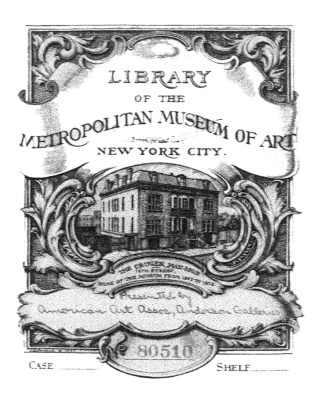

LIBRARY

OF THE

METROPOLITAN MUSEUM OF ART
NEW YORK CITY.

No 80510

CASE _____   SHELF _____

NO PHOTOCOPYING

IN ORDER TO PROTECT THE FRAGILE
PAPER/BINDING OF THIS VOLUME

SALE NUMBER 4145

FREE PUBLIC EXHIBITION

From Saturday, January 12, *to Time of Sale*
Weekdays 9 to 6 · Sunday 2 to 5

PUBLIC SALE

Friday and Saturday
January 18 *and* 19, *at* 2 *p. m.*

EXHIBITION & SALE AT THE

AMERICAN ART ASSOCIATION
ANDERSON GALLERIES · INC

30 East 57th Street
New York City

Sales Conducted by
HIRAM H. PARKE · OTTO BERNET
A. N. BADE · H. E. RUSSELL, JR.

1935

Choice Period Furniture

AUBUSSON AND FLEMISH TAPESTRIES ⚹ BRONZES
EARLY AMERICAN AND GEORGIAN SILVER
AUBUSSON AND ORIENTAL CARPETS
ANTIQUE FABRICS ⚹ LINENS AND LACES ⚹ GLASSWARE
STAFFORDSHIRE, LOWESTOFT, AND OTHER PORCELAINS
PAINTINGS AND DRAWINGS

Property of the Estate of the Late
R. ARTHUR HELLER
Sold by Order of
ARTHUR E. C. HELLER, *Executor*

Property of the Estate of the Late
A. E. NORDEN
Sold by Order of the Surviving EXECUTOR
CITY BANK FARMERS TRUST COMPANY

Property of
MRS. HERBERT L. MAY
Sold by Her Order

The Estate of the Late
J. L. KETTERLINUS
Sold by Order of the Executors
CLARENCE A. WARDEN ⚹ G. L. BISHOP, Jr. ⚹ WALTER WARNER

AND PROPERTY FROM OTHER COLLECTIONS

Public Sale, January 18 & 19, *at* 2 *p. m.*

AMERICAN ART ASSOCIATION
ANDERSON GALLERIES · INC
1935

Priced Catalogues

A priced copy of this Catalogue may be
obtained for One Dollar for each
Session of the Sale

AMERICAN ART ASSOCIATION
ANDERSON GALLERIES · INC

DESIGNS ITS CATALOGUES
AND DIRECTS ALL DETAILS OF ILLUSTRATION
TEXT AND TYPOGRAPHY

Conditions of Sale

[1]

All bids to be PER PIECE as numbered in the catalogue, unless otherwise mentioned.

[2]

The highest bidder to be the buyer. In all cases of disputed bids the lot shall be resold, but the auctioneer will use his judgment as to the good faith of all claims, and his decision shall be final.

[3]

Any bid which is not commensurate with the value of the article offered, or which is merely a nominal or fractional advance, may be rejected by the auctioneer if in his judgment such bid would be likely to affect the sale injuriously.

[4]

The name of the buyer of each lot shall be given immediately after the sale thereof, and when so required, each buyer shall sign a card giving the lot number, amount for which sold, and his or her name and address. ¶ A deposit at the actual time of the sale shall be made of all or such part of the purchase prices as may be required. ¶ If the two foregoing conditions are not complied with, the lot or lots so purchased may at the option of the auctioneer be put up again and resold.

[5]

Title passes upon the fall of the auctioneer's hammer, and thereafter the property is at the purchaser's risk, and neither the owner nor the Company is responsible for the loss of, or any damage to any article by theft, fire, breakage, however occasioned, or any other cause whatsoever.

[6]

Articles not paid for in full and not called for by the purchaser by noon of the day following that of the sale may be turned over by the Company to some carter to be carried to and stored in some warehouse until the time of the delivery therefrom to the purchaser, and the cost of such cartage and storage and any other charges will be charged against the purchaser, and the risk of loss or damage occasioned by such removal or storage will be upon the purchaser. ¶ In any instance where the bill has not been paid in full by noon of the day following that of the sale, the Company reserves the right, any other stipulation in these conditions of sale to the contrary notwithstanding, in respect to any or all lots included in the bill, at its option, either to cancel the sale thereof or to resell the same at public or private sale without further notice for the account of the buyer and to hold the buyer responsible for any deficiency sustained in so doing.

[A]

[7]

Unless the sale is advertised and announced as an unrestricted sale, or a sale without reserve, owners reserve the right to bid.

[8]

The Company exercises great care to catalogue every lot correctly and endeavors therein and also at the actual time of the sale to point out any error, defect, or imperfection, but guaranty is not made either by the owner or the Company of the correctness of the description, genuineness, authenticity or condition of any lot, and no sale will be set aside on account of any incorrectness, error of cataloguing or imperfection not noted or pointed out. Every lot is sold "as is" and without recourse.

[9]

Buying or bidding by the Company for responsible parties on orders transmitted to it by mail, telegraph, or telephone, if conditions permit, will be faithfully attended to without charge. Any purchases so made will be subject to the foregoing conditions of sale. Orders for execution by the Company should be given with such clearness as to leave no room for misunderstanding. Not only should the lot number be given, but also the name of the object, and a bid on several objects catalogued under a single number should be stated to be so much per piece unless the description contains the notation "[Lot.]", in which case the bid should be stated to be so much FOR THE LOT. If the one transmitting the order is unknown to the Company, a deposit must be sent or reference submitted. Shipping directions should also be given.

[10]

All articles sold will be subject, in addition to the purchase price, to the New York City Sales Tax to be paid by the purchaser, unless the purchaser delivers to the Company the requisite certificate that the article was purchased for re-sale.

[11]

The Company will afford every facility for the employment of carriers and packers by the purchasers, but will not be responsible for any damage arising from the acts of such carriers and packers.

[THESE CONDITIONS OF SALE CANNOT BE ALTERED
EXCEPT BY AN OFFICER OF THE COMPANY]

Sales conducted by

HIRAM H. PARKE, OTTO BERNET, A. N. BADE, AND H. E. RUSSELL, JR.
Telephone PLAZA 3-1269 *Cable* ARTGAL *or* ANDAUCTION

·

AMERICAN ART ASSOCIATION
ANDERSON GALLERIES · INC
New York: 30 EAST 57TH STREET

[A]

Order of Sale

FIRST SESSION

FRIDAY AFTERNOON, JANUARY EIGHTEENTH

SECOND AND LAST SESSION
.
SATURDAY AFTERNOON, JANUARY NINETEENTH

[Steinway Grand Piano 547]

[7]

Unless the sale is advertised and announced as an unrestricted sale, or a sale without reserve, owners reserve the right to bid.

[8]

The Company exercises great care to catalogue every lot correctly and endeavors therein and also at the actual time of the sale to point out any error, defect, or imperfection, but guaranty is not made either by the owner or the Company of the correctness of the description, genuineness, authenticity or condition of any lot, and no sale will be set aside on account of any incorrectness, error of cataloguing or imperfection not noted or pointed out. Every lot is sold "as is" and without recourse.

[9]

Buying or bidding by the Company for responsible parties on orders transmitted to it by mail, telegraph, or telephone, if conditions permit, will be faithfully attended to without charge. Any purchases so made will be subject to the foregoing conditions of sale. Orders for execution by the Company should be given with such clearness as to leave no room for misunderstanding. Not only should the lot number be given, but also the name of the object, and a bid on several objects catalogued under a single number should be stated to be so much per piece unless the description contains the notation "[Lot.]", in which case the bid should be stated to be so much FOR THE LOT. If the one transmitting the order is unknown to the Company, a deposit must be sent or reference submitted. Shipping directions should also be given.

[10]

All articles sold will be subject, in addition to the purchase price, to the New York City Sales Tax to be paid by the purchaser, unless the purchaser delivers to the Company the requisite certificate that the article was purchased for re-sale.

[11]

The Company will afford every facility for the employment of carriers and packers by the purchasers, but will not be responsible for any damage arising from the acts of such carriers and packers.

THESE CONDITIONS OF SALE CANNOT BE ALTERED
EXCEPT BY AN OFFICER OF THE COMPANY

Sales conducted by

HIRAM H. PARKE, OTTO BERNET, A. N. BADE, AND H. E. RUSSELL, JR.

Telephone PLAZA 3-1269   *Cable* ARTGAL *or* ANDAUCTION

·

AMERICAN ART ASSOCIATION
ANDERSON GALLERIES · INC
New York: 30 EAST 57TH STREET

[A]

Order of Sale

FIRST SESSION

FRIDAY AFTERNOON, JANUARY EIGHTEENTH

SECOND AND LAST SESSION

SATURDAY AFTERNOON, JANUARY NINETEENTH

[Steinway Grand Piano 547]

First Session

Friday, January 18, 1935, at 2 p.m.

•

Catalogue Numbers 1 to 282 Inclusive

GLASS

1. CORNFLOWER BLUE GLASS FOOTED BOWL
   With flaring folded rim and flaring foot; molded with design of expanded
   spiral ribbing.   *Diameter, 4½ inches*

2. EARLY AMERICAN CLEAR BLOWN FLIP GLASS
   Cylindrical, with slightly flaring sides.   *Height, 4½ inches*

3. AQUAMARINE WASHINGTON AND TAYLOR QUART FLASK
   Flattened ovoid, molded with bust of Washington inscribed *The father of his
   country*, and bust of Taylor inscribed *Genl Taylor*.   *Height, 8½ inches*

4. PAIR ETCHED GLASS DECANTERS WITH SHEFFIELD PLATE COASTERS
   With painted enamel *Port* and *Whiskey* labels.   *Height, 10¾ inches*

5. VIENNESE DECORATED GREEN GLASS TOILET SERVICE
   Five cut glass covered jars with gilded rococo decoration; and three vessels
   with gilded filigree mounts. [Lot.]

6. SERVICE OF GOLD-DECORATED TABLE GLASS
   Six goblets, ten champagnes, three clarets, ten sherries, two ports, seven
   liqueurs, twelve punch cups and saucers, and eleven finger bowls and trays.
   Gilded with rococo foliations. [Lot.] (*May*)

7. LOT OF GOLD-DECORATED TABLE GLASS
   Two ewer decanters with ten quatrefoil clarets; eight sherries; six tinted
   hocks; and ten ruby and emerald tinted hocks with cut stems. [Lot.] (*May*)

8. LOT OF CUT TABLE GLASS
   Ice cream service of oval bowl and fifteen dishes; six whiskey glasses; tray,
   celery bowl, vase, ice bowl; and syrup jug and stand mounted in silver.
   [Lot.] (*May*)

9. PAIR EARLY AMERICAN COBALT BLUE GLASS BOTTLES
   Square, with ribbed sides and octagonal stopper. Slightly imperfect.
                                                                     Height, 8 inches

10. TWO PAIRS PRESSED GLASS COMPOTES   *American, XIX Century*
    Vertically ribbed fluted bowl with grape and flower decoration, on circular
    foot.   *Height, 3 inches*

11. THREE DECORATIVE GLASS AND LUSTRE OBJECTS
English and American, XIX Century
Pair Sandwich sperm oil lamps with pewter burner; and a Staffordshire silver lustre bowl. [Lot.]   *Heights, 3½ and 9½ inches*

12. TWELVE OLD RUBY GLASS GOBLETS
Of late Sandwich type, in diamond pattern. Two sizes. [Lot.]   (*Heller*)

13. PAIR PRESSED GREEN GLASS TABLE LAMPS
Of late Sandwich type, with Godey print parchment shade. (*Heller*)
Height, 16 inches

14. PAIR PRESSED GREEN GLASS TABLE LAMPS
Similar to the preceding. (*Heller*)   *Height, 16 inches*

15. EARLY AMERICAN GREEN GLASS DEMIJOHN, FITTED AS LAMP
Olive green glass demijohn, for two lights. (*Heller*)   *Height, 27 inches*

16. DECORATIVE LOT OF CUT, ENGRAVED, AND TINTED TABLE GLASSWARE
Sweetmeat jar and cover, five decanters, biscuit jar, six green and gold hocks.
[Lot.] (*Norden*)

17. TABLE SERVICE OF ENGLISH CUT CRYSTAL GLASS
Pair of decanters and a pitcher; eleven finger bowls, and twelve plates; ten water goblets, six tumblers, twelve champagnes, twelve clarets, twelve ports, ten burgundies. Cut in diamond and rib pattern; Stourbridge quality. [Lot.]
(*Norden*)

TABLE PORCELAINS

18. TWELVE FINE MINTON SKY BLUE AND GOLD PORCELAIN DEMI-TASSES AND TWELVE SAUCERS
Beautifully decorated with festooned gilded cartouches between etched gold bands.

19. EARLY AMERICAN PAINTED AND LUSTRED CHINA TEA SERVICE
Painted and pink-lustred with flower and leaf vines on white. Twenty-six pieces, one imperfect. [Lot.]   *Height of teapot, 8½ inches*

20. SIX VIENNA HAND-PAINTED PORCELAIN PLATES
Painted with figures of Psyche, Ruth, Sappho, and other famous female characters, within elaborate borders of Renaissance ornament. (*May*)
Diameter, 9½ inches

21. EIGHTEEN LIMOGES DECORATED PORCELAIN PLATES
Ten dinner plates and eight apple green and gold *entrée* plates, with floral decoration. [Lot.] (*May*)   *Diameters, 9¾ and 8¾ inches*

22. TWELVE CHERRY RED AND GOLD PORCELAIN DESSERT PLATES
TWELVE BOUILLON CUPS, AND TEN SAUCERS
Limoges dessert plates with scrolled rim; Austrian porcelain cups and saucers.
[Lot.] (*May*)

23. TWENTY-FOUR GOLD-DECORATED PORCELAIN PLATES
Twelve white and gold luncheon plates; and twelve cream and gold shell-
form oyster plates. [Lot.] (*May*) *Diameter, 8¾ inches*

24. LIMOGES *HAND*-PAINTED PORCELAIN FISH SERVICE
Twelve plates, and sauce boat with stand; painted with fish in their habitat,
signed René, within gilded and apple green border. [Lot.] (*May*)

25. ROYAL COPENHAGEN PORCELAIN SERVICE
Composite part dinner and breakfast service in blue and white; about ninety
pieces. (*Norden*)

26. LOT OF DECORATED TABLE PORCELAINS
*I*ncluding a Limoges gold-decorated service of eleven dinner plates, ten
entrée plates, twelve soup plates, five cups and saucers, vegetable tureen, two
platters, bowl, two relish dishes and sauce tureen; and eighty-six other pieces.
[Lot.] (*May*)

EARLY BLUE STAFFORDSHIRE AND DELFT WARE

27. FOUR EARLY BLUE STAFFORDSHIRE SMALL PLATES *E. Wood and Sons*
Landing of the Pilgrims; and Shirley House, Surrey. Medium blue. [Lot.]
Diameters, 5½ and 6½ inches

28. THREE EARLY BLUE STAFFORDSHIRE PLATES
Landing of the Pilgrims. Medium and light blue. [Lot.]
Diameters, 8½ and 10 inches

29. FOUR EARLY BLUE STAFFORDSHIRE PLATES *Various Makers*
State House, Boston; 'Field Sports'; two others showing fisherman and dog
on river bank. Deep and medium blue. *Diameter, 8½ inches*

30. THREE EARLY BLUE STAFFORDSHIRE PLATES *E. Wood & Sons*
Two showing La *G*range, the residence of the Marquis Lafayette; a view
near Philadelphia. Deep blue. *Diameter, about 10¼ inches*

31. THREE EARLY BLUE STAFFORDSHIRE PLATES *James Clews*
Winter *V*iew of Pittsfield, Mass. Two sizes, deep and medium blue. [Lot.]
Diameters, 7¾ and 8½ inches

32. THREE EARLY BLUE STAFFORDSHIRE PLATES *James Clews*
Winter *V*iew of Pittsfield, Mass. Deep blue, proof condition.
Diameter, 8½ inches

33. EARLY BLUE STAFFORDSHIRE SUGAR BOWL AND SMALL PLATTER
Printed in deep blue with the landing of General Lafayette at Castle Garden, New York. [Lot.]

33A. EARLY BLUE STAFFORDSHIRE *HISTORICAL PLATTER*   *James Clews*
Octagonal oblong platter depicting the landing of General Lafayette at Castle Garden, New York. Printed in deep and medium blue. Almost proof.
Length, 19 inches

34. EARLY BLUE STAFFORDSHIRE COFFEE POT
Decoration of Wilkie subject. Deep blue.   *Height, 10½ inches*

35. NINE BLUE AND WHITE DELFT DISHES   *XVIII Century*
Variously decorated. (*Norden*)   *Diameters, 9 and 10 inches*

36. FOUR BLUE AND WHITE DELFT DISHES   *XVII-XVIII Century*
Two with figural decoration; two floral. One chipped. (*Norden*)
Diameters, 12 and 14 inches

37. PAIR BLUE AND WHITE DELFT TOBACCO JARS   *XVIII Century*
Decorated in cobalt with allegories of the West Indies. From the factory of Bloempot. Old brass covers. (*Norden*)   *Height, 12 inches*

38. FOUR POLYCHROMED DELFT DISHES   *XVII-XVIII Century*
Variously decorated with flower and other motives in cobalt, yellow, green, and *rouge de fer*. [Lot.] (*Norden*)   *Diameters, 9 to 13 inches*

39. PAIR POLYCHROMED DELFT VASES AND A FLOWER *HOLDER*   *Circa 1700*
Vases painted with birds and flowers in the Oriental taste; five-stemmed flower holder somewhat similar. [Lot.] (*Norden*)
Heights, 8½ and 11 inches

40. FINE POLYCHROMED DELFT GARNITURE   *Early XVIII Century*
Three paneled ovoid jars with covers; and a pair of beakers, with covers, painted with flowers in the Oriental taste, in cobalt yellow, green, and *rouge de fer*. Three covers repaired. (*Norden*)   *Height, about 15 inches*
Collection Etienne Delaunoy, Amsterdam

[See illustration]

41. THREE BLUE AND WHITE DELFT DISHES   *XVII-XVIII Century*
Underglaze decoration of birds and flowers in the Oriental taste. (*Norden*)
Diameter, about 14 inches

42. THREE BLUE AND WHITE DELFT DISHES   *XVII-XVIII Century*
Somewhat similar to the preceding. (*Norden*)   *Diameter, about 13 inches*

43. FOUR BLUE AND WHITE DELFT DISHES   *XVII-XVIII Century*
Somewhat similar to the preceding. (*Norden*)   *Diameter, about 13 inches*

LINENS

44. TWO ITALIAN LINEN TABLE CLOTHS, THIRTY-SIX NAPKINS
AND FOUR RUNNERS

Comprising: two cloths, one with a dozen and one with two dozen napkins, and four runners of various lengths; of ecru linen, with cut-work embroidery and lace dies. [Lot.]
    Cloths: 1 yard 32 inches square
    Length, 2 yards 16 inches; width, 1 yard 32 inches

45. THREE BURATTO AND SARDINIAN FILET TABLE CLOTHS
THIRTY-SIX NAPKINS, AND TWO RUNNERS

Cloths in écru Buratto, red filet darned in écru, and amber yellow Sardinian filet; each with a dozen napkins of écru linen; with two écru Buratto runners. [Lot.]

46. YELLOW AND CREAM SATIN DAMASK TABLE CLOTH
AND TWELVE NAPKINS

Patterned with yellow bands bearing roses on a cream ground; twelve napkins to match. Monogrammed. [Lot.]
    Length, 2 yards 15 inches; width, 1 yard 24 inches

47. TWO SATIN DAMASK TABLE CLOTHS AND TWENTY-FOUR NAPKINS

A pink and a matched green cloth in satin damask patterned with medallion of floral vases, each with a dozen napkins; monogrammed. [Lot.]
    Cloth: Length, 2 yards 12 inches; width, 1 yard 31 inches

48. FOUR LINEN DAMASK BRIDGE SETS, TWENTY-FOUR COCKTAIL NAPKINS
AND THIRTY FINGER BOWL DOILIES

Bridge sets in blue, lavender, green, and yellow, monogrammed; two sets of linen cocktail napkins; and eighteen and twelve lace finger bowl doilies. [Lot.]

49. TWO ITALIAN LINEN CLOTHS, TWENTY-FOUR NAPKINS
AND FOUR RUNNERS

Luncheon cloth and tea cloth, each with a dozen napkins, and four runners of assorted lengths; of écru embroidered and cut-work linen. [Lot.]
    Cloths: 1 yard 12 inches square
    Length, 2 yards; width, 1 yard 34 inches

50. THREE SARDINIAN FILET LACE LUNCHEON CLOTHS
AND THIRTY-FIVE LINEN NAPKINS

Two cloths of solid lace, with twelve and eleven napkins matching; one cloth of lace squares between embroidered linen panels, with twelve linen napkins. [Lot.]

1. GREEN SARDINIAN FILET TABLE CLOTH, THREE TEA CLOTHS
AND THREE DOZEN LINEN NAPKINS
Of coarse green filet patterned in écru, one tea cloth centred with green
linen hemstitched in squares; napkins of écru linen with corner insert of green
lace, in three sets of twelve each. [Lot.]

Table cloth: 1 yard 34 inches square

2. ECRU EMBROIDERED AND *HEMSTITCHED* LINEN LUNCHEON CLOTH
AND ELEVEN NAPKINS
Ecru linen hemstitched in squares, with border, central square, and radiating
bands designed with fruit, in embroidered and cut linen joined by *brides
picotées;* together with eleven napkins. [Lot.]

Cloth: 1 yard 17 inches square

[See illustration]

[NUMBER 52]

53. ECRU EMBROIDERED AND *He*MSTITCHED LINEN LUNCHEON CLOTH
AND TWELVE NAPKINS

30- Ecru linen hemstitched in squares, with border and central square of bands
designed with fruit, in embroidered linen joined by *brides picotées;* together
with twelve napkins. [Lot.] Cloth: 2 yards square

54. THREE DOZEN EMBROIDERED ECRU LINEN *Ha*ND TOWELS

20- With blue and tan embroidered and hemstitched borders.

55. THREE DOZEN EMBROIDERED ECRU LINEN *Ha*ND TOWELS

17/6 With blue embroidered and hemstitched borders.

56. FORTY-SIX EMBROIDERED ECRU LINEN *Ha*ND TOWELS

22 5/6 Embroidered and hemstitched in blue and tan. Differing borders. [Lot.]

57. FORTY-SIX EMBROIDERED ECRU LINEN *Ha*ND TOWELS

4 5- Embroidered and hemstitched in blue, and blue and tan. In two sets of
twenty-three towels. [Lot.]

58. TWO ITALIAN LINEN TABLE CLOTHS, THIRTY-SIX NAPKINS
AND FIVE RUNNERS

3 5- Two cloths, one with a dozen and one with two dozen napkins, and five
runners; of écru linen, with cut-work embroidery and punch-work. [Lot.]
Cloths: 1 yard 32 inches, 2 yards 12 inches; width, 1 yard 28 inches

59. TWO ITALIAN LINEN TABLE CLOTHS, TWENTY-FOUR NAPKINS
AND SIX RUNNERS

4 5 Two cloths, each with twelve napkins, and six runners; of écru linen, with
cut-work embroidery and hemstitching. [Lot.]
Cloths: 1 yard 32 inches square and 1 yard 33 inches square

60. LOT OF ECRU EMBROIDERED AND *He*MSTITCHED LINEN TABLE COVERS

70- Fine tea cloth, three tray covers, two medallions, three runners, six tea
napkins, twelve luncheon napkins; design of floral scrollings in embroidered
linen, joined by *brides picotées.* [Lot.]

61. TWO PAIRS EMBROIDERED LINEN SHEETS AND FOUR PILLOW CASES

3 5 Of hemstitched linen, one pair with punch-work embroidery and narrow inset
panels of lace, the other with band of *fil tiré;* each with pair of pillow cases.
[Lot.]

62. TWO PAIRS EMBROIDERED LINEN SHEETS AND SIX PILLOW CASES

27/6 Of hemstitched linen with cut-work embroidery, one pair inset with filet lace,
two and four pillow cases to match. [Lot.]

3. TWELVE EMBROIDERED PERCALE SHEETS AND ELEVEN PILLOW CASES
Six sets of two single sheets and two pillow cases; monogrammed. One set with slight tear and lacking pillow case. [Lot.]

4. TWELVE EMBROIDERED PERCALE SHEETS AND TWELVE PILLOW CASES
Six sets of two single sheets and two pillow cases; monogrammed. [Lot.]

5. TWO PAIRS ECRU LINEN AND LACE BEDSPREADS
Of heavy hemstitched linen with central rectangles of Venetian lace exhibiting leaf scrolls and vases; fringed borders. One pair with pillow coverlets. [Lot.]

6. EIGHT FINE AUSTRIAN WOOL BLANKETS AND THREE SATIN PILLOWS
Six blankets of checkered design, two in lavender, two in yellow, and two in pink; and two double-faced lavender and white blankets. [Lot.]

7. EIGHT FINE AUSTRIAN WOOL BLANKETS AND FOUR SATIN PILLOWS
Double-faced blankets, four in yellow and white, four in pink and white; silk bindings. [Lot.]

8. THIRTY-ONE LACE AND EMBROIDERED LINEN PILLOW CASES
As exhibited. [Lot.]

9. LOT OF ASSORTED TABLE LINENS
Including luncheon, bridge, and tray sets; as exhibited. [Lot.]

EARLY AMERICAN AND OTHER SILVER
AND SHEFFIELD PLATE

0. TWELVE STERLING SILVER-HANDLED DINNER KNIVES AND TWELVE FORKS
Design of crossed laurel festoons; initialed P.

1. TWELVE STERLING SILVER-HANDLED DESSERT KNIVES, TWELVE FORKS AND TWELVE SPOONS
Design of the preceding; initialed P.

2. SEVEN STERLING SILVER-HANDLED FRUIT KNIVES, TWELVE FORKS AND TWELVE SOUP SPOONS
Design of the preceding; initialed P.

3. TEN STERLING SILVER BUTTER KNIVES, TWELVE TEA SPOONS AND TWELVE OYSTER FORKS
Design of the preceding; initialed P.

4. SEVENTEEN STERLING SILVER TEA SPOONS, TWELVE BOUILLON SPOONS AND TWELVE COFFEE SPOONS
Design of the preceding; initialed P.

75. LOT OF STERLING SILVER SERVERS
Including carving set, four cake slices, pair wooden-handled salad servers
and twenty-two other pieces. Design of the preceding. *Initialed* P.

37.2

76. LOT OF SMALL SILVER TABLE ARTICLES
Three cruets, pepperette, two salt spoons. Part of cruets missing. [Lot.]
(*Norden*)

5—

77. SERVICE OF SILVER-PLATED FLATWARE   *Tiffany and Co., New York*
Comprising: twelve table knives, six tablespoons, eleven soup spoons, eleven
table forks. ten dessert forks, nine dessert spoons, eight teaspoons, ten coffee
spoons, eleven butter knives, twelve oyster forks, and six servers. [Lot.]
(*Norden*)

v5—

78. SILVER-FRAMED DRESSING TABLE MIRROR
In the German Renaissance taste. (*Norden*)   *Height, 11 inches*

7.2

79. PAIR STERLING SILVER FLUTED ROSE BOWLS   *George II Style*
Beautiful vertically fluted bowl. with flaring rim and plain foot.
Diameter, 9 inches

90—

80. STERLING SILVER PITCHER, SIX TUMBLER HOLDERS, AND SIX COCKTAILS
Plain silver. initialed P. [Lot.]

50—

81. FOUR STERLING SILVER FLOWER VASES
Reeded pear-shaped vase *repoussé* with festoons of roses.   *Height, 8 inches*

40

82. PAIR CHASED SILVER GOBLETS   *William Gale, New York, circa 1830*
Baluster-shaped, the foot molded with foliage and shells.   *Height, 7½ inches*

45—

83. STERLING SILVER COFFEE SERVICE   *Mauser Mfg. Co., New York*
Tapering cylindrical coffee pot, creamer and sugar bowl, with shell and leaf
scrolled rims. [Lot.] (*May*)

45—

84. REPOUSSÉ STERLING SILVER BREAD TRAY AND TWELVE
BREAD-AND-BUTTER PLATES
Oblong tray with rim *repoussé* with foliations. pierced liner; twelve plates
With a soap box. Monogrammed. [Lot.] (*May*)

60—

85. EARLY AMERICAN SILVER PITCHER
Wood & Hughes, New York, circa 1830
Plain inverted pear-shaped body with curved spout and cylindrical neck
bordered with molded leafage, and bold scrolled handle. With a presentation
inscription to Leffert Lefferts, 1845.   *Height, 9½ inches*
From the Lefferts family of Brooklyn, N. Y.

70

[See illustration on preceding page]

[87]   [85]   [87]
ROW ABOVE: NUMBERS 86–88–89

86. EARLY AMERICAN SILVER SUGAR BOWL
Jos. Loring, Hull and Boston, Mass., circa 1790
Plain oval sugar bowl with reeded edge and two loop handles, and engraved with two garlanded monograms. *Height, 4½ inches*
[See illustration]

87. EARLY AMERICAN SILVER CREAMER AND COVERED SUGAR BOWL
Edw. Watson, Boston, Mass., circa 1830
With bulbous body engraved with pendant leaves, and narrow borders of gadrooning and chased leaf scroll ornament. [Lot.] *Heights, 6 and 8 inches*
[See illustration]

88. EARLY AMERICAN SILVER TEAPOT   *Circa* 1820
Very similar to the preceding in design, but without the leaf engraving; engraved monogram HL. *Height, 7½ inches*
[See illustration]

89. EARLY AMERICAN SILVER CREAMER
Saunders Pitman, Providence, R. I., circa 1790
Of plain silver with engraved monograms, reeded lip, and strap handle.
Height, 4¾ inches

[See illustration on preceding page]

90. SET OF FOUR STERLING SILVER CANDLESTICKS The Gorham Co., New York
Baluster form with urn *bobêche*, and valanced circular foot; *repoussé* with
gadroons and floral ornament. Height, 10¾ inches

91. FOUR SILVER GOBLETS Lincoln & Reed, Boston, circa 1845
Large goblet on molded foot, engraved with a crest and the initials G. MC.
Stamped underneath *Lincoln & Reed, Pure Coin, Boston.* Height, 7½ inches

92. VERY RARE EARLY AMERICAN SILVER SUGAR BOWL AND COVER
BY PAUL REVERE Boston, Mass., 1735-1818
Plain pear-shaped body on molded spreading foot, the domed cover with
flower-shaped finial. Maker's mark stamped underneath: REVERE, shaded
Roman capitals in a rectangle. Height, 5 inches; diameter, 4½ inches

Note: A sugar bowl with cover of almost identical form by Paul
Revere, with embossed decoration and bearing the Chandler arms, is in the
collection of Miss Susanna Willard. *Vide* F. H. Bigelow, *Historic Silver of
the Colonies and its Makers,* Fig. 293.

From the Coffin family of Newburyport, Mass.

[See illustration]

[NUMBER 92]

13. STERLING SILVER COFFEE SERVICE WITH TRAY   Elgin American Mfg. Co.
Coffee pot. creamer. covered sugar bowl. and circular tray of plain silver.
initialed P. [Lot.]   Diameter of tray, 14 inches

14. CHASED STERLING SILVER VASE
Bulbous. chased with iris and monogrammed. (New York Collector)
                                                       Height, 10 inches

15. STERLING SILVER CENTREPIECE   Mauser Mfg. Co., New York
Valanced and reeded circular bowl; repoussé with leaf spirals and floral swags.
With copper liner and plate glass cover.   Diameter, 18 inches

16. SHEFFIELD PLATE OVAL TRAY   Georgian Style
Elegant plain tray with gadrooned edge and two loop handles.
                                                    Length, 27¾ inches

17. PAIR SHEFFIELD PLATE CANDELABRA   Georgian Style
With reeded curved branches for five lights. on fluted columnar stem and
shaped square base. Chased with garlands of flowers.   Height, 26 inches

18. PAIR SHEFFIELD PLATE COVERED ENTRÉE DISHES
                                      The Goldsmiths Co., London
Beaded oval dish and cover in the George III style. with serpent lock handle.
                                                    Length, 12 inches

19. PAIR SHEFFIELD PLATE WINE COOLERS   Georgian Style
Small fluted urn with lion-mask-and-ring handles and paw feet.
                                    Height, 6½ inches; diameter, 6 inches

20. OLD SHEFFIELD PLATE TRAY
Massive tray with engraved escutcheon. bordered with gadrooning and leafage
and with two leaf-scrolled loop handles.   Length, 30½ inches

21. SHEFFIELD PLATE HOT WATER URN   Georgian Style
Fluted vase shape, with loop handles. oval base, and ball feet.
                                                       Height, 11 inches

22. SHEFFIELD PLATE SALVER AND SET OF THREE TEA CADDIES
                                                       XIX Century
Engraved salver bordered with a rococo floral molding; and three plain
graduated oval tea caddies. [Lot.]

EARLY AMERICAN AND ENGLISH FURNITURE
AND DECORATIONS

23. EARLY AMERICAN PEWTER CHARGER
Underside with four maker's touchmarks and name (illegible).
                                                    Height, 16½ inches

104. TWO EARLY AMERICAN AND ENGLISH PEWTER MUGS AND A WICK LAMP
One with English mark. [Lot.] (*Heller*)   Heights, 5½ and 9 inches

12⁵⁰

105. THREE EARLY AMERICAN AND ENGLISH PEWTER LARGE PLATES
One marked 'Boston', one with English mark. (*Heller*)
                                   Diameters, 12 and 14½ inches

20-

106. SIX EARLY AMERICAN PEWTER PLATES
Three with pewterer's touch, three plain. (*Heller*)
                                   Diameter, about 8½ inches

15-

107. THREE OLD ENGLISH PEWTER DISHES
A pair, and one larger. (*Norden*)   Diameters, 13 and 16 inches

15-

108. EIGHT OLD ENGLISH PEWTER PLATES
With London stamp. (*Norden*)   Diameter, about 9 inches

15-

109. FIVE PEWTER PINT MUGS AND TWO COVERED PITCHERS
Covered pitchers of eighteenth century Continental type; mugs modern.
[Lot.] (*Norden*)

22⁵⁰

110. WALNUT TEA CADDY AND PRESSED GLASS WHALE-OIL LAMP
                         English and American, XVIII-XIX Century
Georgian tea casket with bronze trimmings; Sandwich glass etched whale-oil
lamp. [Lot.]   *Heights, 6 and 11½ inches*

22⁵⁰

111. IVORY SCRIMSHAW TUSK   *American, XIX Century*
Engraved with portraits of Grant, Lincoln, and Admiral Farragut, other
figures, and national emblems. Signed U. D. PORTER. (*Heller*)
                                   Length, 25 inches

12⁵⁰

112. TWO AUTOGRAPH LETTERS
One by *Henry W. Longfellow* dated 1866; and one by Oliver Wendell
Holmes, dated 1853; framed with photographs. (*May*)

12⁵⁰

113. HISTORICAL FRAMED CHINTZ WASHINGTON HANDKERCHIEF
                         American, Early XIX Century
Featuring a medallion of Washington standing by his charger surrounded by
thirty-nine stars, with "Washington" and bell above. Also two American
shields on a striped red and white ground. *Height, 24 inches; width, 17 inches*
Collection of Thomas B. Clarke, New York

30

114. LITHOGRAPH   *Currier & Ives, undated*
Trotters on the Snow. Small folio, uncolored. Narrow margin. Signed in
the stone. J. Cameron. Fine clear copy.

12⁵⁰

115. PAINTING ON GLASS OF GEORGE WASHINGTON
After the well known Gilbert Stuart portrait. Gilded frame.
                         Height, 27½ inches; width, 23 inches

30-

TWO OIL PAINTINGS
Frederic Remington, A.N.A.

[NUMBERS 117 (ABOVE) AND 118]

115A. NEEDLEWORK SAMPLER   *American, dated* 1815
Interesting as reflecting the feelings of a disillusioned child named Albinia
Holder. Framed.   *Height,* 19 *inches; width,* 13 *inches*

8 -

FREDERIC REMINGTON, A.N.A.
AMERICAN: 1861-1909
(Oil Painting)

116. 'THERE'LL BE A HOT TIME IN THE OLD TOWN TONIGHT MY BABY'
Full-length figure of a Rough Rider of the Spanish-American War, striding
toward the observer, carrying pack and rifle. Signed at lower right,
FREDERIC REMINGTON. Frame with crossed sabres of the 1st regiment
United States Volunteer Cavalry, Co. K. *Height,* 29 *inches; width,* 19 *inches*

4 v5

FREDERIC REMINGTON, A.N.A.
AMERICAN: 1861-1909
(Oil Painting)

117. "THIS WAS A FATAL EMBARQUATION"
Depicting six Indian braves in a bark canoe paddling across Lake St. Peter,
fleeing from the musket balls of the Iroquois; two savages have been struck
down, another has had his paddle cut in two, while Bailloquet, the Indian fur
trader, stands with his musket in the stern. Signed at lower right, FREDERIC
REMINGTON.   *Grisaille: Height,* 27 *inches; length,* 40 *inches*

4 5 0 -

An illustration for the memoirs of le Chevalier Bailloquet, published by
Remington in *Crooked Trails,* 1898, illus. opp. p. 52. Bailloquet, a Frenchman
living in Canada, was engaged in the fur trade about the middle of the
seventeenth century; he was captured by the Iroquois, and later made his
escape to the Dutch.

[See illustration on preceding page]

FREDERIC REMINGTON, A.N.A.
AMERICAN: 1861-1909
(Oil Painting)

118. "PADDLING THE WOUNDED BRITISH OFFICER"
An episode after the attack upon Ticonderoga, in which a British officer, lying
in the bottom of a bark canoe, attended by his servant, is paddled by two of
Capt. Roger's Rangers dressed in skin and gray duffle hunting frocks; before
a farther bank of rocks and heavy brush. Signed at lower left, FREDERIC
REMINGTON.   *Grisaille: Height,* 27 *inches; length,* 40 *inches*

5 v5

An illustration for an episode from *Joshua Goodenough's Old Letter,*
published by Remington in *Crooked Trails,* 1898, illus. opp. p. 110.

[See illustration on preceding page]

[NUMBER 119]

FREDERIC REMINGTON, A.N.A.
AMERICAN: 1861-1909
(Bronze Group)

9. THE BRONCO BUSTER

Figure of a cowboy astride a rearing bronco, whose mane he grasps with his left hand, while he brandishes a switch in his right hand. Base signed, and inscribed: Copyrighted by Frederic Remington, 1895. Switch missing and tail repaired. Number 55, presumably of the original casting.   *Height, 23 inches*

[See illustration]

[NUMBER 120]

HERMON A. MacNEIL, N.A.
AMERICAN : 1866-
(Bronze Statuette)

120. SIOUX OR BLACKFOOT INDIAN WARRIOR
Standing with arms folded, his shield and bow and arrows slung across
back. Base captioned: Multnomah, and signed H. A. MACNEIL, 1905. F
patina.   *Height*, 38 in
Collection of Thomas W. Lawson, American Art Association, 1923
[See illustration]

400 -

121. GILDED BRONZE AND GLASS PRISM MANTEL GARNITURE
American, XIX Cent
Three-light candelabrum, and pair candlesticks; stems formed as young d
and dog; marble bases. [Lot.] (*Heller*)   *Heights*, 14½ *and* 18 in

30 -

22. SHERATON INLAID MAHOGANY BALLOON CLOCK   *Robert Wood, London*
Inlaid with a sunburst patera and stringing. Striking movement. (*May*)
Height, 26½ inches

23. DERBYSHIRE SPAR URN, FITTED AS LAMP   *Circa* 1800
Beautiful ovoid vase of 'blue John' on square plinth; fitted for electricity,
with shade.   *Height, 26½ inches*

24. PAIR GEORGIAN CUT CRYSTAL LUSTRE CANDELABRA
Prism shaft on knopped base and square foot, with two curved arms for lights,
hung with faceted festoons and lustres.   *Height, 22¼ inches*
From *M. Harris & Sons, London*

25. PAIR COLONIAL BELL METAL ANDIRONS
With ball top and acorn finial, on scrolled splayed legs with claw-and-ball
feet.   *Height, 20 inches*

26. JAPANNED TOLE TEA TRAY   *English, XIX Century*
Decorated with a peacock on a terrace. (*Heller*)   *Length, 30 inches*

27. TWO BRASS SHIP'S LANTERNS AND A TIN LANTERN
American, XIX Century
Brass lanterns by Perkins Marine Lamp Co., Brooklyn; smaller tin lantern;
fitted for electricity. [Lot.] (*Heller*)   *Heights, 13 and 18 inches*

28. GEORGIAN BRASS-TRIMMED IRON WIRE FENDER   *Circa* 1790
Serpentine wire mesh fender capped by narrow brass rail. Good design.
Height, 14½ inches; length, 54 inches

29. INTERESTING PAIR COLONIAL CANNON ANDIRONS, AND TWO FIRE TOOLS
Andirons composed of small bronze ship's cannon barrel on iron cradle with
ball finial and shaft; a long shafted rake and pair tongs with brass ball finials.
[Lot.] (*Heller*)

30. SMALL MIRROR AND TOY BUREAU   *American, XVIII-XIX Century*
Small Chippendale mirror with eagle crest; and miniature bureau with wood
knobs. [Lot.]   *Heights, 21½ and 11 inches*

31. GEORGE III MAHOGANY BRACKET CLOCK
Higgs & Evans, London. circa 1790
Made for the Spanish market. The small molded and fret carved case enclos-
ing ornamented brass tile enscribed with the maker's name, *Higgs y Diego
Evans, Londres.* Striking movement. (*Norden*)   *Height, 17 inches*

32. GEORGIAN INLAID MAHOGANY BAROMETER   *English, XVIII Century*
Upright signpost barometer. The dial bears the name. *Thomas Shaw.*
(*Heller*)   *Height, 38½ inches*

[NUMBER 133]

133. CARVED MARBLE PORTRAIT PLAQUE OF GEORGE AND
MARTHA WASHINGTON   *John Adams Jackson, American: 1825-1879*
Bust portraits in profile approximately life-size, carved in high relief in white
marble. Signed J. A. JACKSON. Mounted in a mahogany fire screen of
Empire design with gilded trimmings.

Dimensions of Plaque: Height, 19½ inches; width, 16½ inches
Dimensions of Screen: Height, 6 feet; width, 31 inches
Note: John Adams Jackson executed busts of Daniel Webster, Wendell
Phillips, and other prominent personages. A group on the reservoir Southern
Gate House, Central Park, New York, is also his work.
Collection of *H. O. Havemeyer*, New York

[See illustration of plaque]

134. MAHOGANY BANJO CLOCK   *Early Federal Style*
With marine decoration on glass front. *(Heller)*   *Height, 37 inches*

[NUMBER 135]

5. RARE INLAID MAHOGANY SHELF CLOCK
David Wood, Newburyport, Mass., circa 1790
Arched domed hood with molded cornice and fret-carved pediment, the rectangular base with columnar pilasters and ogee bracket feet. The maker's name appears faintly on the painted metal dial. Has striking movement. Inlaid with stringings of light woods, and ornamented with brass finials and side handles.   *Height, 33 inches; width, 12 inches*
[See illustration]

6. SET OF WALNUT HANGING SHELVES   *American, XVIII Century*
Frame of three open shelves with two small drawers in the lower part.
Height, 35 inches; width, 25½ inches

7. DECORATED MAHOGANY BANJO CLOCK
Curtis and Sunning, American, circa 1820
Mahogany case with glass front showing the American national emblems and a woodcut of Fallston Springs.   *Height, 40 inches*

138. SMALL DECORATED LEATHER THREE-FOLD SCREEN — *Georgian Style*
Decorated with hunting subjects. — *Height, 40 inches; length, 44 inches*

139. GEORGIAN MAHOGANY CANTERBURY — *English, circa 1800*
Slotted oblong rack with four divisions for magazines or folios, a drawer in
the base. (*Norden*) — *Height, 21 inches; length, 24 inches*

140. MAHOGANY SHELF CLOCK
New Haven Clock Co., New Haven, Conn., circa 1840
Small steeple clock with decorated glass front. (*Heller*) — *Height, 20 inches*
[See illustration with number 223]

141. PINE CELLARETTE AND SMALL CHEST — *American, XVIII Century*
Small rectangular chest with hinged lid, having drawer in the base; and small
oblong chest with a drawer in the lower part. [Lot.]
Heights, 22 and 20 inches; widths, 16 and 21 inches

142. HISTORICAL PAINTED SIDE CHAIR. FORMERLY OWNED BY
ABRAHAM LINCOLN — *American, Early XIX Century*
Solid-seated small chair with splatted back and ring-turned spindle legs and
stretchers; coated with black paint. (*Heller*)

*Note: A document tacked under the seat reads as follows: "Washington,
D. C., May 24, 1920. This dining room chair was sold to a citizen of Spring-
field, Illinois, by Mr. Lincoln previous to his departure to Washington, D. C.
to be inaugurated President of the United States. Mr. Lincoln did not set a
price on his furniture, but let the people pay him what they thought they were
worth. This chair and another like it, were purchased from the man while I
was living in the Lincoln Homestead from 1883-1893. (Signed) O. H.
Oldroyd."*

[See illustration of chair and document]

143. MAHOGANY AND MAPLE BEDSIDE TABLE — *American, circa 1815*
Square top with two drawers in fiddle back maple; turned, tapering legs.
(*Heller*) — *Height, 29 inches; width, 19 inches*

144. CHIPPENDALE CARVED MAHOGANY ARMCHAIR — *English, XVIII Century*
Of ample proportions, with interlaced strap splat, voluted open arms and
square stretchered legs; slip seat. (*May*)

145. HEPPLEWHITE INLAID MAHOGANY PEMBROKE TABLE
American, Late XVIII Century
Rectangular top with two hinged leaves; one drawer. Tapering square legs
and frieze banded with light woods. Top chipped.
Height, 28 inches; length open, 34½ inche.

146. COMB-BACK WINDSOR ROCKING CHAIR — *American, XVIII Century*
With saddle-shaped seat, turned straddle legs. (*Heller*)

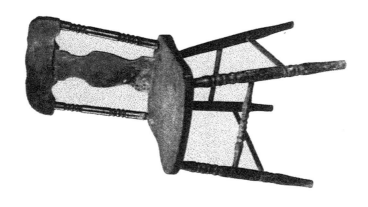

147. CHIPPENDALE CARVED MAHOGANY WALL MIRROR
Frame fret-carved at top and base, the crest ornamented with a gilded metal American eagle and shield.   *Height, 36 inches; width, 15½ inches*

148. PINE AND CHERRY DISH-TOP TRIPOD TABLE   *American, XVIII Century*
Circular top on turned pedestal and snake-footed cabriole tripod. (*Heller*)
Height, 27 inches; diameter, 22 inches

149. LATE SHERATON INLAID MAHOGANY WORK TABLE   *English, circa 1815*
Hinged shaped top fancifully inlaid uncovering box-like small compartments in amboyna wood; on pedestal and triangular base with brass paw feet.
Height, 28 inches; width, 23 inches

150. CHIPPENDALE MAHOGANY SLANT-TOP DESK   *American, XVIII Century*
Body contains four beaded drawers, above which a hinged slant flap encloses a series of small drawers and arched pigeonholes and, at the centre, a door with secret drawers; on tapering bracket feet.
Height, 43 inches; width, 42 inches

[See illustration]

[NUMBER 150]

1. WINDSOR WRITING CHAIR *American, Early XIX Century*
Square back and curved arms filled with small bulbous spindles, the arms
strengthened with metal brace. (*Heller*)

2. SHERATON CHERRY TILTING CANDLESTAND *American, circa 1800*
Square top with indented corners tilting on club pedestal and cabriole tripod.
Height, 28 inches; width, 19 inches

3. HEPPLEWHITE CHILD'S INLAID CHERRY SLANT-TOP DESK
Contains four drawers in the front, above which a hinged flap encloses small
drawers and pigeonholes. Inlaid and banded with light wood.
Height, 30 inches; width, 23½ inches

4. DUNCAN PHYFE CARVED MAHOGANY UPHOLSTERED LOVE SEAT
American, XIX Century
Small settee, the straight back carved with drapery swags and gadroon motive,
reeded sloped arms extended into reeded tapering legs. Covered in green and
gold brocatelle. Loose seat cushion. *Length, 48 inches*

5. DECORATED SATINWOOD VITRINE TABLE *Sheraton Style*
Quartrefoil-shaped glazed top with silk-lined interior.
Height, 28 inches; width, 17 inches

6. SHERATON MAHOGANY SWELL-FRONT BUREAU *American, circa 1810*
Curved front contains four beaded drawers with repoussé brass knobs: fluted
pilasters at corners extending into tapering round supports.
Height, 39 inches; length, 40 inches

7. EARLY GEORGIAN MAHOGANY DRESSING TABLE *English, XVIII Century*
Small oblong table with drawers, and shell-carved cabriole legs with club feet.
(*Norden*) *Height, 25 inches; length, 27 inches*

8. PAIR CARVED MAHOGANY SIDE CHAIRS *American, circa 1830*
Late Empire type, with upholstered seat. (*Heller*)

9. HEPPLEWHITE INLAID MAHOGANY AND SATINWOOD CARD TABLE
American, Late XVIII Century
Hinged shaped top, the frieze banded with branch satinwood; on tapering
square legs with string inlay. *Height, 29 inches; length open, 35 inches*

10. TWO WINDSOR ARM CHAIRS *American, Early XIX Century*
Flaring square back filled with spear-pattern and spindle slats; one fitted with
rockers. Loose cushions. (*Heller*)

[NUMBER 161]   [NUMBER 162]

161. HEPPLEWHITE INLAID MAHOGANY SMALL TABLE

Baltimore, Late XVIII Century

Small oblong table with drawer and tapering square legs; the top, frieze, and legs attractively inlaid with stringings of light woods.

Height, 27 inches; width, 24 inches

[See *illustration*]

162. QUEEN ANNE WALNUT FIDDLE-BACK SIDE CHAIR

American, XVIII Century

Slatted open back, saddle-shaped slip seat in green damask, Dutch-footed cabriole front legs, and turned stretchers.

[See illustration]

163. CHIPPENDALE CARVED MAHOGANY WALL MIRROR

American, XVIII Century

Frame fret-carved at top and base and with gilded eagle ornament.

Height, 38 inches; width, 18 inches

[NUMBER 164]

CHIPPENDALE UPHOLSTERED MAHOGANY WING CHAIR
                                    American, XVIII Century
Attractive chair in vine-pattern chintz, on mahogany grooved square legs and
stretchers.
                        [See illustration]

MAPLE AND BIRCH TRIPOD TABLE   *American, XVIII Century*
Circular top tilting on vase-shaped pedestal and snake-footed cabriole tripod.
(Heller)   *Height, 27 inches; diameter, 29 inches*

MAHOGANY SERPENTINE-FRONT BUREAU   *American, XVIII Century*
Gently undulating front containing four drawers with Chippendale brasses;
the edge of the slightly overlapping top banded with string inlay. Molded
base and ogive bracket feet.   *Height, 33 inches; length, 41 inches*

167. IMPORTANT CARVED MAHOGANY 'CURVED ARM' SOFA

Duncan Phyfe, New York, circa 1800-10

Sheraton model, the horizontal crest rail divided into three panels featuring formalized groups of wheat ears and darts tied with ribbon, carved in low relief. The reeded and sloped arms curved gracefully inward, terminating on reeded and leaf-carved balusters; the seat frame and four tapering front legs also reeded, the back legs plain and slightly canted. Upholstered and covered in striped buff fabric. *Length, 6 feet 6 inches*

Cf. Charles O. Cornelius, *Furniture Masterpieces of Duncan Phyfe*, 1922, Pl. XII

[See *illustration*]

168. THREE CHIPPENDALE MAPLE RUSH-SEATED SIDE CHAIRS

American, XVIII Century

Country type chair with openwork splat, rush seat, and grooved straight legs.

169. INLAID MAHOGANY BEDSIDE TABLE *American, Late XVIII Century*

Shaped square top, one drawer, tapering square legs. (*Heller*)

Height, 28 inches; width, 21 inches

170. SHERATON INLAID MAHOGANY SLANT-FRONT DESK

American, XIX Century

Three drawers, and hinged flap enclosing drawers and pigeonholes.

Height, 44 inches; width, 36 inches

171. HICKORY, MAPLE, AND PINE COMB-BACK WINDSOR ARM CHAIR

American, XVIII Century

Flaring tall back with seven spindles, rounded pine seat, and turned straddle legs with stretchers.

172. INLAID MAHOGANY LIQUEUR CABINET, IN THE SHERATON TASTE

Banded with satinwood. Equipped with glass decanters and tumblers.

Height, 30 inches; width, 23 inches

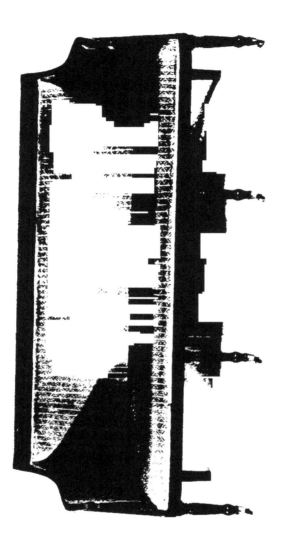

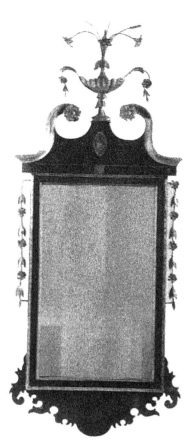

[NUMBER 173]

173. HEPPLEWHITE INLAID AND PARCEL-GILDED MAHOGANY WALL MIRROR
American, circa 17

Beautiful mirror of New York type, the upright rectangular frame outlin
with gilded moldings, its scrolled crest terminating in rosettes and surmount
by an urn of wheat ears and flowers; at the sides, pendent sprays of flow
and laurel; the base fret-carved in scroll outline. Frame inlaid with fillets
light and dark woods, while below the urn is an oval medallion of shells a
leafage in tinted marquetry. *Height, 58 inches; width, 23 inc*
Collection of Capt. Harry Butler Stannard, Guilford, Conn.

[See illustration]

74. HEPPLEWHITE INLAID AND PARCEL-GILDED MAHOGANY WALL MIRROR
                                   American, circa 1790
Companion to the preceding.   *Height, 58 inches; width, 23 inches*
Collection of Capt. Harry Butler Stannard, Guilford, Conn.

75. WALNUT TAVERN TABLE   *American, Early XVIII Century*
Oblong top overlapping four vase-and-ring-turned supports with plain
stretchers. One drawer.   *Height, 25½ inches; length, 38 inches*

76. SHERATON PINE BUREAU   *American, Late XVIII Century*
Chest of three beaded drawers with molded oval brasses, dentiled frieze, and
curved bracket feet. (*Heller*)   *Height, 38 inches; width, 40 inches*

77. DECORATED SATINWOOD CHINA CABINET   *Adam Style*
With mirrored interior and glazed doors, two solid doors below enclosing
shelves.   *Height, 6 feet 2 inches; width, 40 inches*
From Duveen Bros., New York

78. SET OF SIX ELM WOOD 'GOTHIC' WINDSOR ARM CHAIRS
Arched high back with pierced splats in the Gothic taste, saddle-shaped seat,
club-footed cabriole legs with stretchers. (*Norden*)

79. SMALL CHERRY AND CURLY MAPLE TABLE   *American, circa 1815*
Square top with two drawers on spirally turned legs. (*Heller*)
                            Height, 27 inches; width, 21 inches

80. HEPPLEWHITE CARVED MAHOGANY ARM CHAIR   *American, XIX Century*
Open shield back and grooved supports, worn leather seat.

81. PINE AND CHERRY DROP-LEAF TABLE   *American, XVIII Century*
Rectangular three-leaf top on six tapering square legs. (*Heller*)
                       Height, 28 inches; length open, 40 inches

82. GEORGE II CARVED MAHOGANY SIDE CHAIR   *English, XVIII Century*
Pre-Chippendale chair with carved openwork splat and paw-footed cabriole
front legs. Upholstered seat.

83. CHIPPENDALE SHELL-CARVED MAHOGANY SIDE CHAIR
WITH CLAW-AND-BALL FEET   *Philadelphia, Mid-XVIII Century*
Open back with voluted and shell-carved crest, upholstered slip seat, and
cabriole front legs terminating in claw-and-ball feet. Repair on back of
openwork splat.

84. SHERATON INLAID MAPLE DRESSING TABLE   *American, circa 1800*
Bow front contains a drawer in bird's-eye maple and mahogany, tapering
square legs with cuffed feet.   *Height, 29½ inches; length, 36 inches*

185. QUEEN ANNE INLAID WALNUT BUREAU   *English, XVIII Century*
Case of five drawers veneered in figured walnut and banded with light wood
marquetry. (*Norden*)   *Height, 37 inches; length, 38 inches*

186. CARVED MAHOGANY CLAW-AND-BALL FOOT LOWBOY
        American, XIX Century
In the style of William Savery, with seven drawers, and carved shell ornament on front and supports.   *Height, 32 inches; length, 34 inches*

187. SHERATON INLAID MAHOGANY AND SATINWOOD SETTEE
        American, circa 1800
Straight back banded with satinwood, sloped arms terminating in reeded and
leaf-carved balusters, four dainty reeded tapering front legs. Covered in green
fabric.   *Length, 6 feet 11 inches*

188. MAHOGANY OCCASIONAL TABLE   *American, circa 1800*
Small square table with drawer and tapering square legs.
        Height, 25 inches; width, 17 inches

189. HEPPLEWHITE INLAID MAHOGANY PEMBROKE TABLE
        English, XVIII Century
Oval top banded with tulipwood, on four tapering and inlaid square legs.
One drawer.   *Height, 29 inches; length, 39 inches*

190. GEORGE III CARVED OAK LONG-CASE CLOCK
        Benjamin Barlow, Ashton-under-Lyne, XVIII Century
Molded oak case with scrolled and domed hood having three brass finials;

richly mounted and engraved dial of brass and silvered metal, showing phases
of the moon and bearing the legend: *Time Takes Wings and Flies Away.*
        Height, 7 feet 6 inches

191. CHIPPENDALE MAPLE RUSH-SEATED ARMCHAIR
        American, XVIII Century
Slightly flaring back with openwork splat, curved arms, turned frontal posts,
and plain stretchers.

193. QUEEN ANNE MAPLE WALL MIRROR
Molded frame with fretted shaped cresting. (*Heller*)
        Height, 36 inches; width, 14 inches

194. EARLY GEORGIAN MAHOGANY ROUNDABOUT CHAIR
        English, XVIII Century
Corner chair of *Hogarth* type, the seat recovered in green leather.

[NUMBER 195]

195. HEPPLEWHITE INLAID MAPLE SWELL-FRONT BUREAU
American, Late XVIII Century
Four drawers in bird's-eye maple banded with mahogany, inlaid valanced skirt and tapering bracket feet. Good specimen.
Height, 36½ inches; length, 38 inches
[See illustration]

196. PINE AND MAPLE TAVERN TABLE   *American, XVIII Century*
Widely overlapping square top on vase-turned straddle legs with turned feet.
Height, 26 inches; length, 30 inches

197. CARVED CHERRY DUTCH-FOOTED HIGHBOY BASE
American, XVIII Century
With four drawers showing carved fan at centre, and pad-footed cabriole legs. Furnished with new top.   *Height, 33 inches; length, 44 inches*

198. EARLY PINE AND MAPLE SCHOOLMASTER'S DESK *American, XVIII Century*
Oblong top with gallery, slant-front disclosing painted small drawers and recesses, on deep valanced frieze with quadrangular tapering legs.
Height, 36½ inches; width, 25½ inches

199. MAPLE HIGH CHEST OF DRAWERS *American, XVIII Century*
Case of five long drawers with molded overlapping top, on valanced base with bracket feet. *Height, 47 inches; width, 41½ inches*

200. TWO PAINTED ROCKING CHAIRS *American, Early XIX Century*
Stenciled *Hitchcock* chair, and child's arm rocker. **(Heller)**

201. PAINTED PINE AND MAPLE CIRCULAR TAVERN TABLE
American, XVIII Century
Circular top on vase-turned slender straddle legs, with plain stretcher. Retains old paint. *Height, 24½ inches; diameter, 20 inch.*

202. GEORGIAN CRYSTAL GLASS CHANDELIER
Entirely of glass elaborately hung with festoons of lustres and pendants and with curved branches supporting flower-shaped sconces for twelve light. Fitted for electricity. **(Norden)** *Height, 5 feet 6 inch*

203. PINE AND MAPLE WINDSOR WRITING CHAIR *American, circa 18*
Bamboo-pattern spindles, a drawer below the writing arm. Reconditioned

204. MAPLE AND PINE TRIPOD TABLE *American, XVIII Century*
Circular dish top on club-shaped pedestal and cabriole tripod.
Height, 25 inches; diameter, 20 inc

205. EARLY GEORGIAN CARVED MAHOGANY AND PARCEL-GILDED WALL MIRROR
English, XVIII Century
Shaped frame outlined with gilded and plain moldings; rosette-decorated top. Eagle ornament restored. *Height, 48 inches; width, 26 inc*

206. GEORGIAN CRYSTAL GLASS CHANDELIER
Of Sheraton design, composed of a bronze circlet supporting eight urn-shaped sconces suspended on numerous festoons of glass lustres. Fitted for electric. **(Norden)** *Height, 49 in*

[NUMBER 207]

7. SET OF SEVEN HEPPLEWHITE FINELY CARVED AND INLAID MAHOGANY
SHIELD-BACK SIDE CHAIRS   *American, Late XVIII Century*
Beautiful chair, the molded shield back framing an openwork splat of interlaced vase design carved with husk sprays, clusters of wheat ears, and a small
rosette, converging at the base to a sunburst motive, also inlaid with rosette
motives in light woods. Upholstered seat, molded tapering square front legs
with spade feet, and stretchers.

[See illustration of two]

8. MAPLE DUTCH-FOOT TAVERN TABLE   *American, XVIII Century*
Oblong top overlapping one drawer, the four tapering round legs ending in
pad feet.   *Height, 27½ inches; length, 30 inches*

9. SIX CARVED MAHOGANY SIDE CHAIRS   *American, circa 1840*
In late Empire style, with mohair slip seat.

210. HEPPLEWHITE INLAID MAHOGANY BOW-FRONT SIDEBOARD

American, circa 1790

Outcurved front containing a deep drawer at centre with let-down front and fitted for writing purposes, flanked by a drawer and a cupboard. With molded oval sunburst brasses. On six tapering square legs inlaid and banded with light woods. *Height, 42 inches; length, 5 feet 7 inches*

[See illustration]

211. HEPPLEWHITE CARVED MAHOGANY SIDE CHAIR *American, XVIII Century*

Philadelphia type, the arched back framing an openwork beaker-form splat carved with wheat ears. Upholstered seat, grooved tapering front legs with spade feet; one leg spliced.

212. GEORGIAN MAHOGANY TILTING OVAL BREAKFAST TABLE

English, circa 1800

Oval top tilting on turned pedestal and splayed tripod with brass feet. *Height, 27 inches; length, 43 inches*

213. PINE AND MAPLE TAVERN TABLE *American, XVIII Century*

Cleated oblong top on vase-turned slender legs with plain stretchers. *Height, 25 inches; length, 29½ inches*

214. POKER-WORK CHEST *English (?), XVII Century*

The front elaborately intaglio-carved with allegorical figures and grotesques. *Height, 25 inches; length, 50 inches*

215. GEORGIAN CARVED AND GILDED CONVEX MIRROR

Circular frame surmounted by cresting of spread eagle and acanthus scrolls. (*Heller*) *Height, 39 inches*

216. SHERATON CARVED MAHOGANY DRESSING TABLE *New York, circa* 1810

In two parts; with six beaded drawers and leaf-carved corner pilasters extending into reeded supports with undershelf and paw feet. Surmounted by rectagular swivel mirror. *Height, 5 feet 5 inches; width, 38 inches*

217. LATE SHERATON INLAID MAHOGANY SIDE CHAIR *American, circa* 1815

Rectangular back and tapering square legs inlaid with satinwood lines. Seat upholstered.

218. PINE AND MAPLE TAVERN TABLE *American, Early XVIII Century*

Overlapping oblong top on four vase-turned legs with plain stretchers. *Height, 25½ inches; length, 31 inches*

219. THREE EARLY AMERICAN RUSH-SEATED MAPLE SIDE CHAIRS

Simple chair with slatted back; one with rockers. (*Heller*)

22

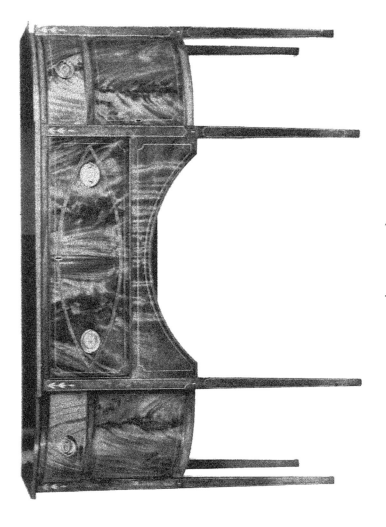

[NUMBER 220]

220. CHIPPENDALE CARVED MAHOGANY TRIPOD TABLE WITH SCALLOPED TOP
English, XVIII Century
Tilting circular top with molded scalloped edge, on turned tapering pedestal and shell-carved cabriole tripod with claw-and-ball feet.
Height, 27 inches; diameter, 32 inches
[See illustration]

1 4/0

221. CURLY MAPLE SLANT-FRONT DESK   American, XVIII Century
Four long drawers in fiddle-back maple, and hinged flap enclosing small drawers and pigeonholes.   Height, 42 inches; width, 39 inches

8 0

222. TWO SLAT-BACK MAPLE SIDE CHAIRS   American, XVIII Century
With rush and splint seats; one with rockers. (Heller)

1 0

[NUMBERS 140 AND 223]

FIGURED MAPLE BUREAU   *American, circa* 1815
Rectangular chest of two small and four long drawers in fiddle back and
bird's-eye maple; baluster-pattern stiles extending into turned short legs.
Uncommon and attractive piece. (*Heller*)

Height, 38 inches; length, 42 inches

[See illustration]

PINE HUTCH TABLE   *American, XVIII Century*
Oblong top tilts back forming settle with box seat with hinged lid and slightly
shaped supports.   *Height, 30 inches; length, 42 inches*

225. SHERATON MAHOGANY SIDEBOARD WITH SHAPED FRONT *American, 1800-10*
Shaped front with convex centre section equipped with five shallow drawers
above three cupboards and two deep bottle drawers faced in nicely figured
mahogany. Front ornamented with hollow and full fluted stiles extending
into four reeded tapering legs which end in brass paw feet; below the top
at either end, a pull-out shelf. Augmented towards the end of the last century
with a mahogany and brass gallery. *Height, 43 inches; length, 6 feet 8 inches*

226. SMALL CARVED MAPLE SCROLL-TOP HIGHBOY   *American, XVIII Century*
In two parts, containing nine drawers with carved fan motive at top and
bottom; molded broken arch cornice with three urn finials, valanced skirt
and short cabriole legs. Reconstructed.
                    Height, 5 feet 3½ inches; width, 34 inches

227. TURNED BIRCH LOW POST BEDSTEAD   *American, circa 1810*
Four club-and-pineapple posts of even height, shaped headboard, and plain
rails.   *Height, 5 feet; width, 48 inches*

228. SHERATON MAPLE FIELD BEDSTEAD   *American, circa 1800*
The footposts finely turned in vase baluster pattern, the head posts and support domed tester frame with white cotton tester. Posts ornamented with brass
urn finials. With box spring.   *Height, 5 feet 7 inches; width, 4 feet 7 inches*

229. HAND-WOVEN WOOL SPREAD EAGLE COVERLET   *American, dated 185-*
Good specimen, featuring stars and acanthus wreaths surrounded by American
eagles and other patriotic emblems in coral red and white. Reversible.
                    Length, 7 feet 6 inches; width, 7 feet 6 inches

230. HAND-WOVEN WOOL COVERLET   *Pennsylvania, dated 184-*
In red and white, woven with a star centring floral motives and inscribed
Made by C. Wiand, Allentown, 1849. Length, 8 feet; width, 6 feet 6 inches

231. EARLY AMERICAN HOOKED RUG
Wreaths and posies of bright colored blossoms in a light buff ground. Needs
repair.   *Length, 5 feet 8 inches; width, 2 feet 7 inches*

232. EARLY AMERICAN HOOKED CARPET
Attractive pattern of colorful groups of blossoms and leaves distributed over
an ivory field. Border of large brown leaf arabesque motives edged in black
                    Length, 9 feet; width, 8 feet 7 inches

233. PINE LONG-CASE CLOCK   *American, Late XVIII Century*
Simple pine case with arched pediment and cut-out base, fancifully painted
wood dial, and wood works. (*Heller*)   *Height, 7 feet 7 inches*

[NUMBER 234]   [NUMBER 235]

MAPLE, HICKORY, AND PINE COMB-BACK WINDSOR ARMCHAIR
                                        American, XVIII Century
Tall bow and comb back composed of seven spindles; rounded seat, bamboo-turned legs and stretchers.
                        [See illustration]

MAPLE AND PINE OVAL BUTTERFLY TABLE   American, 1700-1720
The top consists of a stationary leaf and two hinged leaves supported on pivoting solid brackets doweled into the longitudinal stretchers; four slightly straddle legs with vase turnings. A drawer at one end of the frame. Retains old dark paint.   Height, 25 inches; length open, 34 inches
                        [See illustration]

THREE MAPLE SIDE CHAIRS   American, Early XIX Century
Late Windsor and Sheraton type, one in curly maple. (Heller)

PINE OVAL HUTCH TABLE   American, XVIII Century
Oval top widely overlapping the square box frame; tilts back forming a chair, with shaped supports and chamfered shoes.
                        Height, 28½ inches; length, 53 inches

238. BIRD'S-EYE MAPLE AND CHERRY BUREAU   *American, circa* 1815
Front containing four beaded drawers with wood knobs, flanked by turned
pilasters extending into turned short legs. (*Heller*)
                                Height, 43½ *inches; length,* 42 *inches*

239. PINE AND MAPLE TAVERN TABLE   *American, Early XVIII Century*
Rudely constructed country-type table with three-board top, columnar supports, and one drawer. (*Heller*)   *Height,* 27 *inches; length,* 47 *inches*

240. INLAID MAHOGANY BRASS DIAL LONG-CASE CLOCK
                        Simon Willard, Roxbury, Mass., circa 1795
Tall case with brass-mounted chamfered and reeded corners, the molded
pendulum door and the base inlaid with segmented fans or sunbursts at the
corners in light and dark woods. Domed and fretted hood with brass-mounted
pilasters, two ball finials, and a gilded metal bird central finial. Arched dial
of brass with pewter hour ring and subsidiary dial, decorated with gilded
spandrel mounts engraved with the maker's name; phases of the moon on a
painted revolving disc. Brass-dialed Willard clocks are exceedingly rare.
                                  Height, 7 *feet* 10 *inches*
Collection of Louis Guerineau Myers, American Art Association-Anderson
    Galleries, 1932
                [See illustration]

241. CARVED MAHOGANY THREE-CHAIR-BACK SETTEE   *Hepplewhite Style*
Triple-shield-back carved with 'Prince of Wales' feathers and drapery swags;
grooved tapered square legs with stretchers. Seat in crimson damask.
                                Length, 5 *feet* 4 *inches*

242. PINE TABLE   *American, XVIII Century*
Probably a workman's table, having two drawers, broad top, and plain end
supports. (*Heller*)   *Height,* 31 *inches; length,* 42 *inches*

243. MAPLE SEAT-BACK ARMCHAIR   *American, XVIII Century*
Plain back posts with turned finials and four arched slats, frontal posts and
stretchers nicely turned; rush seat.

244. PINE HUTCH TABLE   *American, XVIII Century*
Wide seven-board top tilting backwards forming a settle, fastened to the frame
with wood pegs. Good patina. (*Heller*)   *Height,* 28 *inches; length,* 5 *feet*

[NUMBER 240]

245. HEPPLEWHITE MAHOGANY SERPENTINE-FRONT SIDEBOARD
English, XVIII Century
Gently undulating front contains two deep bottle drawers flanking a shallow cutlery drawer, below which is a sliding tambour shutter; six tapering square legs with spade feet. *Height, 36 inches; length, 5 feet 6 inches*
[See illustration]

246. MAPLE SEAT-BACK ARMCHAIR *American, Early XVIII Century*
Composed of turned posts with mushroom front finials, four arched slats, and rush seat.

247. LATE SHERATON CARVED AND GILDED OVERMANTEL MIRROR
American, circa 1815
Three-paneled mirror with baluster pattern frame.
Height, 24 inches; length, 54 inches

248. WALNUT TWO-DRAWER BLANKET CHEST *American, XVIII Century*
Finely constructed rectangular chest with iron strap hinges and end handles, two drawers in the lower part and bracket feet. (*Heller*)
Height, 29 inches; length, 50 inches

249. QUEEN ANNE MAPLE HIGHBOY *American, Mid-XVIII Century*
Five long drawers in the upper part, above one long drawer, and three smaller in the lower body, the centre drawer carved with fan medallion; on cabriole legs ending in pad feet. *Height, 6 feet; width, 40 inches*

250. CURLY MAPLE LOW POST BEDSTEAD *American, XIX Century*
With turned low posts, shaped headboard with spool-turned crest, and rope slats. With mattress and hangings. (*Heller*)
Height, 41 inches; width, 52 inches

251. PAIR CARVED MAHOGANY SINGLE BEDSTEADS *Duncan Phyfe Style*
The head and foot panels carved with wheat ears and ribbon knots. Furnished with box spring. *Height, 51 inches; width, 44 inches*

252. PINE HUTCH TABLE *American, XVIII Century*
Square top tilting backwards to form a chair. (*Heller*)
Height, 26 inches; length, 41 inches

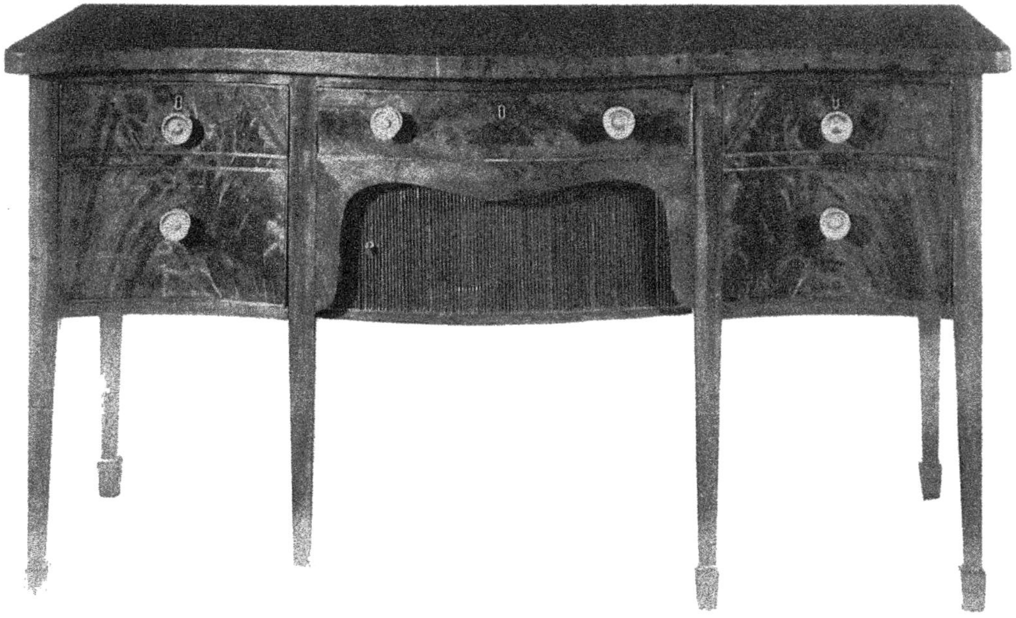

[NUMBER 245]

KINDLY READ CONDITIONS OF SALE IN FOREPART OF CATALOGUE

253. QUEEN ANNE CURLY MAPLE HIGHBOY   *American, Mid-XVIII Century*
Upper carcass in rich tawny striped maple containing seven drawers, the lower
body with four drawers and featuring fine carved fan at centre, above a skirt
cut in lunette pattern; on cabriole legs with pad feet.

/ 4⁄o

Height, 6 feet 2 inches; width, 40 inches

[See illustration]

254. MAHOGANY CORNER CABINET   *American, circa 1815*
With glazed doors enclosing the upper part, solid doors at the base, and
7⁄o   scrolled pediment.   *Height, 8 feet; width, 40 inches*

255. SET OF TEN CARVED MAHOGANY DINING CHAIRS *American, XIX Century*
Two arm- and eight side chairs, in the Colonial Chippendale taste. With
slip-in seats.

[NUMBER 253]

256. QUEEN ANNE INLAID BURL WALNUT SECRETARY WITH MIRROR DOORS
English, Early XVIII Century
The upper cabinet with shelves and compartments enclosed by two arched
beveled mirror doors, surmounting base with four drawers and hinged slant
flap enclosing pigeonholes and small drawers. Banded with herringbone
ornament. *Height, 7 feet 8 inches; width, 39 inches*

[See illustration]

257. JACOBEAN CARVED OAK TWO-DRAWER CHEST *English, XVII Century*
Paneled front and sides elaborately carved with conventional tulips and vines,
two drawers in the base. *Height, 35 inches; length, 53 inches*

258. WILLIAM AND MARY TURNED OAK TABLE *English, Late XVII Century*
Oblong top with drawer, on spirally turned legs with saltire stretcher.
(*Norden*) *Height, 29 inches; length, 33 inches*

259. CARVED MAHOGANY HIGH-POST BEDSTEAD *American, XIX Century*
Pour tall posts carved with pineapple and acanthus design. With tester frame
furnished with box spring, mattress, and hangings. (*Heller*)
Height, 8 feet 4 inches; width, 5 feet 2 inches

260. TWO EARLY AMERICAN TURNED MAPLE LOW-POST BEDSTEADS
With attractively turned corner posts, shaped headboard. With wire spring,
mattress, and hanging. (*Heller*) *Height, 47 inches; width, 41 inches*

261. SANTO DOMINGO MAHOGANY WRITING TABLE *American, circa 1825*
Late Empire style, equipped with small and large drawers with cupboard and
a leather-lined writing slide. In two parts.
Height, 44 inches; length, 47 inches

[NUMBER 256]

262. QUEEN ANNE OAK DRESSER   *English, XVIII Century*
Open-faced dresser of so-called Welsh type with shelves and cupboards
the upper part, three drawers below; short club-footed cabriole legs. (*Nord*
Height, 6 feet 6 inches; width, 6 feet 2 inche

[See illustration]

263. BOW-BACK WINDSOR ARMCHAIR AND SIDE CHAIR *American, XVIII Century*
Armchair with rounded seat, side chair with saddle seat; turned straddle leg·
and stretchers. [Lot.]

264. TWO SMALL MAPLE AND PINE TABLES   *American, Early XIX Century*
One with drawer, one with straddle legs. (*Heller*) *Width, about 17 inche*

265. MAPLE AND HICKORY LADDER-BACK ARMCHAIR *American, XVIII Century*
Tall back with turned finials and five curved slats, rush seat, turned frontal
posts and stretchers.

266. LATE GEORGIAN CARVED AND GILDED PIER MIRROR   *American, circa 182*
Upright frame composed of balusters and acorn-decorated pediment carve·
with anthemia and shells.   *Height, 59 inches; width, 33 inche*

267. INLAID MAHOGANY AND CIRCASSIAN WALNUT BUREAU
                                          American, XIX Century
Shaped front with four long drawers with pressed glass knobs, banded wit·
light woods.   *Height, 42 inches; length, 44 inche*

268. TWO TURNED MAPLE LOW-POST BEDSTEADS   *American, XIX Century*
Almost a pair, with turned corner posts and shaped headboard. Wire sprin·
and mattress, and hangings. (*Heller*)   *Height, 36 inches; width, 42 inche*

269. TWO TURNED MAPLE TRUNDLE BEDS   *American, XIX Century*
With low corner posts and rope slats. Furnished with mattress. (*Heller*)
                                      Width, about 42 inche

270. MAHOGANY BOOKCASE   *American, XIX Century*
Enclosed by two glazed doors with interlaced mullions, on claw-and-ball fee·
                            Height, 5 feet 5 inches; width, 56 inche

271. MAPLE AND HICKORY COMB-BACK WINDSOR SIDE CHAIR
                                          American, XVIII Century
Handsome specimen with conforming flaring back, saddle seat, vase-and-bul·
turned straddle legs and stretchers.

272. TWO SMALL MAPLE TABLES   *American, Early XIX Century*
Square top with drawer and turned tapering legs. (*Heller*)
                                      Width, about 21 inche

[NUMBER 262]

Blue Staffordshire Ware Selected from Numbers 27—34

273. UPHOLSTERED MAHOGANY ARM ROCKER   *American, Mid-XIX Centur*
      With swanneck arms, covered in Jacquard tapestry.

274. PAIR LATE GEORGIAN BRASS ANDIRONS AND TWO FIRE TOOLS
      [Lot.] (*Norden*)   *Height of andirons, 22 inch*

275. LOT OF IRON AND STEEL FIREPLACE FURNISHINGS
      Two pairs ball-top andirons, steel poker, shovel and tongs, spark guard, an
      an old wire mesh fire guard. [Lot.] (*Norden*)
                                                  Height of andirons, 15 and 18 inch

276. GEORGIAN PIERCED BRASS FENDER
      Oblong, vertically pierced and engraved, urn finials at corners. (*Norden*)
                                                  Length, 60 inch

277. LOT OF COLONIAL IRON AND BRASS *HEARTH UTENSILS*
      Pair gooseneck iron andirons, long-shafted rake, two tongs, broiler, tw
      toasting forks, two pot scales, and three ladles. [Lot.] (*Heller*)

278. TWO PAIRS GEORGIAN IRON AND BRASS ANDIRONS
      Iron and steel shaft with brass urn finial; and two wire mesh spark guard
      [Lot.] (*Norden*)   *Heights, about 24 inch*

279. EARLY AMERICAN WARMING PAN AND SMALL MIRROR
      Brass and turned maple warming pan, maple-framed small mirror. [Lot
      (*Heller*)

280. TWO COLONIAL *HAND HEWN* WOOD OX YOKES
      Interesting relic of a primitive mode of transportation. (*Heller*)

281. GILDED METAL EAGLE WEATHER VANE AND BURL BIRCH BOWL
                                          American, XVIII Centu
      Hand-fashioned birch bowl; and gilded spread eagle weather vane of lat
      period. [Lot.]

282. SIX EARLY AMERICAN COPPER VESSELS
      Kettle, bucket, three pitchers and a jar. [Lot.] (*Heller*)

[END OF FIRST SESSION]

Second and Last Session

Saturday, January 19, 1935, at 2 p. m.

·

Catalogue Numbers 283 to 563 Inclusive

CHINESE AND ORIENTAL LOWESTOFT PORCELAINS

TWO BOWLS *K'ang-hsi and Ch'ien-lung*
Decoration in underglaze and overglaze colors. (*Norden*)
Diameters, 7 and 8 inches

TWO JARS AND A BEAKER-FORM VASE *Ch'ien-lung and Tao Kuang*
Ovoid celadon jar; blue and white bronze-form beaker, and hawthorn jar.
[Lot.] (*Norden*) *Heights, 9 and 10 inches.*

TURQUOISE BLUE BOTTLE *Ch'ien-lung*
With laterally streaked deep turquoise glaze; stand. (*Norden*)
Height, 6 inches

TWO RETICULATED BLUE AND WHITE WINE POTS *Yung Chêng*
In the Persian taste, with *ajouré* body simulating honeycomb; cover also
pierced. (*Norden*) *Height, 8½ inches*

POWDER BLUE BALUSTER VASE *Ch'ien-lung*
Of inverted pear shape, gilded with pagodas and lake scenes.
Height, 10 inches

THREE-COLOR POTTERY JARDINIÈRE *Ming*
Oblong receptacle on pierced plinth, molded with small figures, sceptre heads,
and leafage; glazed orange, turquoise, and green.
Height, 12½ inches; length, 14 inches

TWO NANKING BLUE AND WHITE DISHES *K'ang-hsi*
One showing flowers in radiating panels; the other peonies, rocks, and butter-
flies. (*Norden*) *Diameter, 14½ inches*

TWO NANKING BLUE AND WHITE DISHES *K'ang-hsi*
Underglaze decoration of flowers in radiating panels. (*Norden*)
Diameter, 15 inches

NANKING BLUE AND WHITE DISH *K'ang-hsi*
Decoration of Flowers of the Seasons, peacocks, and arabesques. Rim chipped.
(*Norden*) *Diameter, 18½ inches*

292. FAMILLE VERTE WINE POT　　　　　　　　　　　　　*K'ang-hi*

Ribbed melon-shaped small vessel with short spout and fluted cover. Richly decorated in *famille* verte colors heightened with gold, with the 'antique' objects in shaped panels surrounded by chrysanthemums, peonies, and leaf arabesques. The square-looped handle striped aubergine and yellow simulating wicker work. (*Norden*)　　　　　　　　　　　*Height, 7¾ inches*

293. ORIENTAL LOWESTOFT PORCELAIN CREAMER WITH BLUE AND
GOLD STAR BORDER　　　　　　　　　　　　*Late XVIII Century*

Helmet-shaped with branch handle, the rim decorated with gold stars on blue band; below the spout, a representation of the arms of New York.

Height, 4½ inches

294. ORIENTAL LOWESTOFT PORCELAIN TWO-HANDLED URN　　*XVIII Century*

Ovoid urn on square foot, two open handles. Molded in relief with husk festoons and medallions, and painted with landscape vignettes, flowers, and swags in India ink, apricot, and gold. Cover repaired.　　*Height, 15 inches*

[See illustration]

[NUMBER 294]　　　　　　　　　[NUMBER 295]

5. ORIENTAL LOWESTOFT PORCELAIN ARMORIAL DISH   XVIII Century
The centre and border skilfully painted in India ink, colors, and gold with
Dutch landscape and marine vignettes, and armorial shield and crest.
                                                    Diameter, 11½ inches
                    [See illustration]

6. PAIR ORIENTAL LOWESTOFT ARMORIAL DISHES   Early XVIII Century
Finely decorated in colored enamels and gold with a coat of arms and panels
of flowers within gold arabesque borders. (Norden)   Diameter, 13½ inches

7. ORIENTAL LOWESTOFT ARMORIAL DISH   XVIII Century
Decorated with a Dutch coat of arms with quarterings within a running
border of rocaille shells and scrolls. Rim chipped. (Norden)
                                                    Diameter, 12½ inches

8. TWO ORIENTAL LOWESTOFT PORCELAIN ARMORIAL PLATTERS ·
                                                    Late XVIII Century
Oval, with cobalt blue double border, the centre with a coat of arms in colors.
Repaired.   Length, 14½ inches

9. ORIENTAL LOWESTOFT PORCELAIN TEA SERVICE   Late XVIII Century
Assembled set: two cylindrical teapots with covers, sugar bowl and cover,
creamer and cover, helmet-shaped milk pitcher, tea caddy and cover, waste
bowl, saucer dish, teapot stand, eleven saucers, eleven teacups, and seven coffee
cups. Decorated with bands of diaper ornament in India ink. Some have
wood stands. A few pieces imperfect. [Lot.]

GEORGIAN SILVER

10. GEORGE III SILVER SOUP LADLE   London, circa 1770
Plain circular bowl and tapering stem with monogram. (New York Collector)   Length, 12 inches

11. GEORGE II SILVER SOUP LADLE   London, circa 1750
Shell-pattern bowl with stem engraved with baroque foliations and flowers,
and crested. (New York Collector)   Length, 15 inches

12. TWO QUEEN ANNE SILVER RAT-TAIL TABLESPOONS   London, circa 1709
One has date letter for the above date, the other bears maker's mark: G V, a
fleur de lis and crown above. (New York Collector)   Length, 7½ inches

13. GEORGE III SILVER CREAMER   London, 1792
Helmet-shaped, with beaded rim, loop handle, and square base. Handle repaired. (New York Collector)   Height, 6½ inches

304. PAIR GEORGE III SILVER OBLONG SALTS

G. Cooper and Co., Sheffield, circa 182

Urn-shaped with half-fluted body, molded gadroon border, and blue glas liner. (New York Collector) Length, 3¾ inch

30 -

305. GEORGE III SILVER CREAM JUG London, 181

Oblong with horizontally ribbed plain body, gadrooned rim, and reede handle. Monogrammed. (New York Collector) Length, 5¼ inch

45 -

306. RARE CHARLES I SILVER SEAL-TOP SPOON London, circa 163

Egg-shaped bowl stamped with crowned leopard's head in a shaped shiel Six-sided stem with three stamps on reverse and terminating in chiseled sea top. Engraved initials I C. (New York Collector) Length, 6¾ inch

120 -

307. SET OF FOUR GEORGE III GILDED SILVER DESSERT SPOONS London, 178

Handsome large spoon with plain bowl and tapering stem with bright c feather edge. Maker's mark W C. (New York Collector)

20 -

308. THREE GEORGIAN PLAIN SILVER TUMBLER CUPS

London, 1727, circa 1750 and 17

Small plain round cups, one engraved with initials on base. Two have part illegible marks. Heights, 1¾ to 2¼ inch

50 -

309. SET OF FOUR GEORGE III ADAM SILVER SALTS

Robert and Thomas Makepeace, London, 17

Three salts bear the marks of the above date and maker, the fourth made match at a later date. Circular bowl on three reeded curved legs and cla and-ball feet, and circular base with reeded edge. Interior gilded. Small cre (New York Collector) Diameter, 3¼ inch

[See illustration of two]

110 -

310. GEORGE III SILVER SHAPED TEA CADDY Thomas Hemming, London, 1

Handsome small 'Chippendale' caddy of square baluster form, the corners a base molded with strapwork, shells, and gadroon ornament, the cover wi pineapple finial. (New York Collector) Height, 5¾ inc

[See illustration]

60 -

311. PAIR GEORGE II PLAIN SILVER SAUCEBOATS

William Shaw and William Priest, London, 17

Beautiful oval body with scalloped flaring rim, plain except for engrav monogram on one side; open scroll and acanthus handle. Three fluted she and-scroll legs. (New York Collector) Length, 6¾ inc

[See illustration]

240 -

[310]

BERS 309, 313, 314, 312, 309

304. PAIR GEORGE III SILVER OBLONG SALTS

G. Cooper and Co., Sheffield, circa 1820

Urn-shaped with half-fluted body, molded gadroon border, and blue glass liner. (*New York Collector*) *Length, 3¾ inches*

30 –

305. GEORGE III SILVER CREAM JUG *London,* 1815

Oblong with horizontally ribbed plain body, gadrooned rim, and reeded handle. Monogrammed. (*New York Collector*) *Length, 5¼ inches*

45 –

306. RARE CHARLES I SILVER SEAL-TOP SPOON *London, circa* 1635

Egg-shaped bowl stamped with crowned leopard's head in a shaped shield. Six-sided stem with three stamps on reverse and terminating in chiseled seal top. Engraved initials I C. (*New York Collector*) *Length, 6¾ inches*

120 –

307. SET OF FOUR GEORGE III GILDED SILVER DESSERT SPOONS *London,* 1780

Handsome large spoon with plain bowl and tapering stem with bright cut feather edge. Maker's mark W C. (*New York Collector*)

20 –

308. THREE GEORGIAN PLAIN SILVER TUMBLER CUPS

London, 1727, circa 1750 *and* 1794

Small plain round cups, one engraved with initials on base. Two have partly illegible marks. *Heights, 1¾ to 2¼ inches*

50 –

309. SET OF FOUR GEORGE III ADAM SILVER SALTS

Robert and Thomas Makepeace, London, 1794

Three salts bear the marks of the above date and maker, the fourth made to match at a later date. Circular bowl on three reeded curved legs and claw-and-ball feet, and circular base with reeded edge. Interior gilded. Small crest. (*New York Collector*) *Diameter, 3¼ inches*

[See illustration of two]

160 –

310. GEORGE III SILVER SHAPED TEA CADDY *Thomas Hemming. London,* 1764

Handsome small 'Chippendale' caddy of square baluster form, the corners and base molded with strapwork, shells, and gadroon ornament, the cover with pineapple finial. (*New York Collector*) *Height, 5¾ inches*

[See illustration]

60 –

311. PAIR GEORGE II PLAIN SILVER SAUCEBOATS

William Shaw and William Priest, London, 1755

Beautiful oval body with scalloped flaring rim, plain except for engraved monogram on one side; open scroll and acanthus handle. Three fluted shell-and-scroll legs. (*New York Collector*) *Length, 6¾ inches*

[See illustration]

240 –

[311]

[310]

[311]

ROW ABOVE: NUMBERS 309–313–314–312–309

312. GEORGE III SILVER MUFFINEER London, circa 1760
Plain bulbous body with rope-pattern border, latticed pierced top with flame
finial. Small monogram. (*New York Collector*) *Height, 5¼ inches*

40 - [See illustration on preceding page]

313. GEORGE II SILVER MUFFINEER London, 1757
Plain bulbous body with reeded borders, the top pierced and engraved in
conventional pattern. (*New York Collector*) *Height, 5 inches*

40 - [See illustration on preceding page]

314. RARE QUEEN ANNE PLAIN SILVER CASTER London, circa 1705
Plain bulbous body, the top finely pierced with arabesques and strapwork
Marked on cover and base. Small engraved crest. Maker's mark: A D in
shaped shield. (*New York Collector*) *Height, 6 inche*

120 - *Cf.* Charles J. Jackson, *English Goldsmiths and Their Marks*, 1921, P. 485
[See illustration on preceding page]

315. GEORGE III SILVER SALVER London, 180
Reeded octagonal tray with engraved cartouche and scrolled border band, o
four feet. *Length, 10¼ inch*

60 -

316. GEORGE III SILVER AND CUT GLASS INKSTAND
John Watson, Sheffield, 180
Plain oval tray on four bell-form feet; fitted with three cut glass inkwells, or
65 - topped by a taper stick. (*Norden*) *Length, 8¼ inch*

317. TWELVE GEORGE III SILVER TABLESPOONS *Alexander Barnet, London*, 178
Heavy plain spoon, fully hall-marked, the tapering stem monogrammed. On
30 - of slightly earlier date. (*New York Collector*)

318. EIGHT GEORGE III SILVER TABLESPOONS John Lautier, London, 17.
Similar in pattern to the preceding. Fully hall-marked. Stem monogramme
22 - (*New York Collector*)

319. TWELVE GEORGE III SILVER TABLE FORKS London, 1783 and 17.
Plain four-pronged fork. Fully hall-marked. Stem crested. (*New Yo*
27 - Collector)

320. TWELVE GEORGE III SILVER DESSERT FORKS
Thomas Northcote and George Bourne, London, 17.
Similar in pattern to the preceding. Fully hall-marked. Stem crested. (*N*
York Collector)

[322]   [323]   [324]

ROW ABOVE: NUMBER 321

GEORGE III SILVER TEA SERVICE
                    R. & S. Hennell & John Angell, London, 1808-15
Teapot, creamer, and sugar bowl; squat oblate body encircled by a collar band
of gadrooning. Assembled set, of good quality. [Lot.]
                    [See illustration]

SILVER INKSTAND IN THE GEORGIAN TASTE   *London,* 1880
Chamfered oblong stand with winged claw feet, and fitted with festooned
inkwells and stamp box surmounted by a finial lamp.   *Length,* 11 *inches*
                    [See illustration]

SILVER HOT WATER KETTLE ON STAND   *London,* 1881
Gadrooned skittle-ball kettle with reeded spout and wicker-wrapped bail
handle; on stand on four shell feet and with spirit burner.
                    Height, 12½ *inches*

                    [See illustration]

324. GEORGE III SILVER COVERED TANKARD   *Hester Bateman, London, 17*
Plain cylindrical tankard with dome top and leaf-scrolled handle; engrav
monogram.   *Height, 6¼ inch*
[See illustration on preceding page]

100-

325. GEORGE II SILVER SHAPED TANKARD   *London, 17*
Slightly bulbous body encircled by molded band, stepped dome cover wi
open thumb piece, S-scroll handle engraved with initials J M R, molded flari
base.   *Height, 8 incl*

90-

326. GEORGE IV SILVER CHAMBER CANDLESTICK WITH SNUFFER
John and Thomas Settle, Sheffield, 18
Oblong, with urn-shaped sconce and loose conical snuffer, the borders mold
with shells and gadroon ornament. (*New York Collector*) *Width, 6½ inci*

50

327. SMALL GEORGE IV SILVER COMMUNION CHALICE AND PATEN
London, 18
Small chalice and circular paten, plain except for engraved symbols of a
*H*ost. Small crest. (*New York Collector*)
Height of chalice, 4 inches; diameter of paten, 3½ inc

60

328. PAIR GEORGE III SILVER BOAT-SHAPED SALTS
William Simmons, London, 17
Plain oval bowl on spreading oval foot, the edges molded and reeded. Ra
(*New York Collector*)   *Width, 4 inc*

60-

329. GEORGE III SILVER CANDLE SNUFFERS AND TRAY   *London, 1790 and 18*
Plain scissors-patterned snuffers, with reeded borders; oblong tray w
gadroon border and monogrammed centre. (*New York Collector*)
Length of tray, 8½ inc

40-

330. SMALL GEORGE III SILVER SPHERICAL TEAPOT   *Newcastle, 1*
Plain body encircled by gadroon bands; tapering curved spout, and three l
feet. (*New York Collector*)   *Length, 9 inc*

25-

331. GEORGE III PLAIN SILVER SMALL OVAL CHEESE TRAY
Crespin Fuller, London, 1
Plain except for small engraved crest near border, the edges and loop han
reeded. Rare. (*New York Collector*)   *Length, 12 in.*

65-

332. PAIR ADAM SHEFFIELD PLATE CANDELABRA   *Circa 1*
Faceted round tapering stem with urn *bobêche*, supporting two spir
twisted arms for lights and three reeded urn *bobêches*.
Height, about 16½ in

90-

;. GEORGE III SILVER SHAPED TEA CADDY
Thomas Hemming, London, 1765
Handsome small 'Chippendale' caddy, of oblong baluster form, the shoulders
and base molded with shells, strapwork, and gadroon ornament; cover with
pineapple finial. (*New York Collector*)   *Height, 5½ inches*

.. GEORGE III SILVER SHAPED TANKARD   *John Kentenber, London, 1770*
Slightly bulbous body encircled by molded band, domed hinged cover with
pierced thumbpiece, molded spreading foot. Engraved coat of arms.
Height, 8 inches

;. GEORGE III SILVER AND CRYSTAL GLASS CRUET STAND
J. W. Story and W. Elliott, London, 1820
Silver circular stand, the borders, handle, and feet molded with gadroon and
shell ornament; contains four crystal glass cruet bottles, two having silver
labels. (*New York Collector*)   *Height, 9 inches*

;. IMPORTANT GEORGIAN SILVER TWO-HANDLED TEA TRAY
Richard Sibley, London, 1820
Beautiful heavy silver oval tray, the centre plain except for engraved monogram and escutcheon in a cartouche; the border molded with gadroon ornament; loop handles with acanthus and reeding. On four feet molded as shells
and lion's claws. Weight, about 128 ounces. (*New York Collector*)
Length, 26 inches

[See illustration]

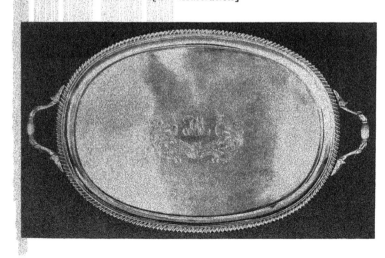

[NUMBER 336]

337. PAIR GEORGE III PLAIN SILVER OVAL PLATTERS

William Bateman, London, 1812

200- Heavy silver oval platter, with plain centre, the edge molded with gadroon ornament, a small engraved crest on the border. Very fine quality. (New York Collector)

Length, 15½ inches

338. PAIR REPOUSSÉ SILVER ALTAR CANDLESTICKS   *Italian, XVIII Century*

15— Of wood, faced with a plate of silver *repoussé* with flutings and Louis XVI festoon ornament.

Height, 19 inches

BROCADES, VELVETS, DAMASKS, AND A
RUSSIAN SABLE CAPE

338A. RUSSIAN SABLE CAPE

100— Hip-length wrap of superbly matched skins, with short round collar and trimmed with a border of tails. In excellent condition; lined with gray silk brocade.

Length, 24 inches

339. FOUR CUSHIONS

15— In amber damask, appliqué-embroidered velours, and buff silk. [Lot.]

340. FRENCH NEEDLEPOINT CIRCULAR COVER

15— *Tête de nègre* ground, worked with bands of leaf scrollings in colors.

Diameter, 39 inches

341. TWO BROCADE PANELS   *Italian, XVIII Century*

15— Louis XV panel patterned with flowers on yellow ground; striped red and white panel in Directoire pattern with delicate flower vines. Worn. [Lot.]

Length, about 6 feet; width, about 5 feet

342. ORANGE SILK BROCADE TABLE COVER   *Persian, XVIII Century*

12.50 With diagonal design of a perched parrot on a floral sprig, in gold and colored silks.

Length, 33 inches; width, 30 inches

343. CRIMSON SILK DAMASK AND SEVENTEENTH CENTURY POINT D'HONGRIE EMBROIDERY BANNER

2.50 Damask with scrolling floral design, inset with a small panel of Florentine silk embroidery.

Length, 5 feet 4 inches; width, 39 inches

344. SILK BROCATELLE COPE AND BROCADE CHASUBLE   *French, XVIII Century*

15— Amber yellow cope patterned with leaves and flowers; Nattier blue brocade chasuble patterned with small colored flowers and trimmed with gold galloon. Cope imperfect. [Lot.]

TWO SILK BROCADE TABLE COVERS   French, XVIII Century
Brick red gold brocade, worn; and rose pink silk brocade. Both with small
allover floral patterns.   *Lengths, 41 and 37 inches; widths, 31 inches*

DRAP D'OR AND SEVENTEENTH CENTURY GARNET VELVET BANNER
Centre panel of cloth-of-gold, with a floral pergola design picked out in red;
bordered with antique velvet banded with silver galloon.
                              Length, 5 feet 9 inches; width, 46 inches

RÉGENCE GREEN SATIN DAMASK COVERLET French, Early XVIII Century
Somewhat faded; trimmed with silk cord fringe of later date.
                              Length, 8 feet; width, 8 feet

APRICOT VELVET COVERLET   French, Late XVIII Century
Velvet of fluctuating tone, in fine preservation; banded in gold galloon.
                        Length, 7 feet 6 inches; width, 5 feet 7 inches

RÉGENCE YELLOW SATIN DAMASK COVERLET French, Early XVIII Century
Somewhat faded and worn; trimmed with silk cord fringe of later date.
                              Length, 9 feet; width, 8 feet

PAIR FINE IVORY SILK BROCADE COVERLETS . *Spanish XVII Century Style*
Richly woven in gold thread and shaded brown, rose, blue, and green silks
with festooned garden architecture. Lined and flounced.
                        Effective length, 6 feet 3 inches; width, 39 inches

SILK AND SILVER BROCADE COPE   *Spanish, Early XVIII Century*
Patterned with blossoms and trailing vines and jardinières on an ivory ground
trimmed with gold fringe and galloon.

GOLD- AND SILK-EMBROIDERED ROSE TAFFETAS COVERLET
                              Turkish, XVIII Century
Embroidered with arabesqued vines of flowers and ferns, enriched with
sequins.   *Length, 58½ inches; width, 54 inches*

RUBY VELVET *HANGING* AND TABLE RUNNER   *XVIII-XIX Century*
Banded in gold galloon, the hanging fringed. [Lot.]
                        Length, 5 feet 7 inches; width, 56 inches
                        Length, 5 feet 9 inches; width, 12½ inches

EMPIRE PLUM VELVET PANEL   French, circa 1810
Composed of four strips, and trimmed with gold galloon. Lined.
                        Length, 7 feet 7 inches; width, 7 feet

FRENCH AND ITALIAN FURNITURE
AND DECORATIONS

355. MINIATURE ON IVORY   *French. XIX Century*
20-   Danae and Cupid. Gilded frame.   *Width, 5½ inches*
Collection of William Salomon, American Art Association, 1923

356. TWO SMALL BRONZE MORTARS   *Spanish, XVII-XVIII Centuries*
15-   One cast with mascarons, the other with illegible date. (Norden)
                     Diameter, about 4½ inches

357. BRONZE BUST AND PAIR RENAISSANCE ANIMAL STATUETTES
22   Bust of Frederick of Prussia; and a pair of finely modeled crouching leopard
    figurines of the German Renaissance. [Lot.]

358. LIMOGES BRONZE AND CHAMPLEVÉ ENAMEL PORTFOLIO AND INKSTAND
                                Romanesque Style
70-   Beautifully enameled with figures of crusader and lion hunter, the portfolio
    with diaper border inset with semi-precious cabochons. Together with a pen
    tray. [Lot.]

359. PAIR CARL ZEISS BINOCULARS AND CASE OF LIQUEUR BOTTLES
4-   Binoculars and bottles in cowhide cases. One monogrammed. [Lot.]
0-   (Norden)

360. PAIR ITALIAN RENAISSANCE BRONZE CANDLESTICKS AND
    PAIR CENTAUR STATUETTES
4-   Rearing figures of centaurs, on vert antique marble bases; and pair of kneeling
    bearded candlestick figures. [Lot.]   *Heights, 6½ and 9¼ inches*

361. MARBLE AND BRONZE DORÉ MANTEL CLOCK
80   Enamel dial painted with a landscape, flanked by small *bronze doré* figures
    on yellow Siena and *vert antique* marble base.   *Height, 8½ inches*

362. PAIR DIRECTOIRE DECORATED TOLE URNS AND COVERS
65-   Vase-shaped, with lion-mask and ring handle and pointed cover, the decoration
    of classical figures *en grisaille* on yellow and gold ground. *Height, 13 inches*

363. LOT OF DECORATIVE BRASS OBJECTS
4-   Three pairs of candlesticks; old Dutch engraved brass tray; tobacco box; an
0-   a barrel-shaped tobacco jar. (Norden)

364. LAPIS LAZULI CIGAR BOX
95-   Beautifully veneered with lapis and lined as humidor.   *Length, 9½ inch*

;. DECORATIVE PORCELAIN MANTEL CLOCK, AND AN ORNAMENT
Paris porcelain clock with gilded bronze mounts; and Royal Worcester
nautilus. [Lot.]   *Heights, 9 and 15 inches*

i. PAIR OF DECORATED PORCELAIN TABLE LAMPS   *K'ang-hsi Style*
Famille verte decoration. Wired for three lights.   *Height, 25 inches*

'. TEN STAINED AND PAINTED GLASS MARINE VIGNETTES
                                        Dutch, XVIII Century
Featuring English and Dutch men-of-war in oval medallions, leaded as small
oblong window panes. (*Norden*)   *Height, 11 inches; width, 8½ inches*

\. FOUR STAINED AND PAINTED GLASS PANELS *Dutch, XVII-XVIII Century*
Two featuring SS Henricus and Katerina. Pair with Teniers figure subjects
in monochrome. (*Norden*)   *Height, about 14 inches*

\. LILLE DECORATED FAIENCE PLATTER
With pastoral subject after Boucher.   *Length, 17 inches*

\. PAIR PARIS DECORATED PORCELAIN VASES, FITTED AS LAMPS
Painted with floral medallions and sprigs; fitted for electricity, with silk
shades.   *Height, 14 inches*

. IVORY CIGARETTE BOX, MOUNTED IN BRONZE DORÉ   *Renaissance Style*
Engraved with Renaissance ornament and mounted with gilded bronze band-
ings and tiny putto figures; fitted as humidor.   *Length, 12½ inches*
From E. F. Caldwell & Co., New York

. GILDED BRONZE EQUESTRIAN STATUETTE
                            Jean Léon Gérome, French: 1824-1904
Napoleon as First Consul astride a caparisoned charger and doffing his hat.
Cast by Siot, Paris. Signed.   *Height, 17 inches; width, 15 inches*

. BRONZE GROUP   *P. E. Delabrierre, French: XIX Century*
Bull, cow, and calf grouped on rocky oval base with sprouting fungus. Signed.
                                            Length, 22 inches

A. BRONZE STATUETTE   *Ron Sauvage, French: XIX Century*
Venus de Milo, after the antique. Signed.   *Height, 24 inches*

B. GILDED BRONZE STATUETTE
                    Désiré-Pierre-Louis Marie, French: XIX Century
Muse. Draped female figure seated with lyre at her feet. Signed.
                                            Height, 22 inches

374. LOUIS XV BRONZE DORÉ AND DECORATED PORCELAIN PENDULE
Causard, Paris
Chinoiserie clock in the form of an oval canopy, with base of porcelain and bronze doré supports hung with bells. A fine reproduction.
Height, 15½ inches
[See illustration with number 459]

375. BRONZE STATUETTE   *Frederick W. MacMonnies, N.A., American:* 1863-
Diana. Nude lissome figure of the young goddess in running attitude, holding a bow. Circular base signed, F. MACMONNIES, 1890. Copyright 1894. Repaired. (*Norden*)
Height, 19 inches

376. PAIR BRONZE PUTTO GROUPS   *After Pigalle*
Three chubby putti tumbling over each other in play; round statuary marble bases.   *Heights, 10¼ and 11 inches*
[See illustration with numbers 421 and 422]

·AUGUSTE RODIN
FRENCH: 1840-1917
(Bronze Group)

377. THE KISS
Nude figures of a youth and maiden embracing, seated upon a rock. Signed RODIN. Apparently a posthumous cast.   *Height, 10 inches*

378. ROMAN SILVER LAMP
Fluted urn form in the classic style, with four lights, standard handle, and curved reflector arm. Fitted for electricity.   *Height, 30½ inches*

379. PAIR BRONZE DORÉ AND LAPIS LAZULI BUSTS   *Louis XVI Style*
Bewigged figures of nobles, mounted as herms, on lapis bases.
Height, 13½ inches
From E. F. Caldwell & Co., New York
[See illustration with number 462]

380. BRONZE PUTTO GROUP   *After Pigall*
Figures of a Bacchic faun and putto with a bunch of grapes, sprawling on lion's skin; round statuary marble base.   *Height, 9¼ inches*

381. PAIR GEORGIAN LEAD GARDEN STATUETTES
Small nude figures of infants seated upon sphere bases. (*Norden*)
Height, 15 inch

2. LOUIS XVI MARBLE AND BRONZE DORÉ LYRE CLOCK
                    E. F. Caldwell & Co., New York
Statuary marble beautifully mounted, on yellow Siena marble foot.
                                        Height, 15 inches

3. LIMOGES BRONZE AND CHAMPLEVÉ ENAMEL CASKET AND
PHOTOGRAPH FRAME   *Romanesque Style*
The casket enameled with figures of a noble and lady playing lutes, the frame
inset with K'ossu gold tapestry; adorned with enamel escutcheons and semi-
precious cabochons. [Lot.]

4. BRONZE STATUETTE   *Directoire Style*
Standing figure of a maiden, on statuary marble plinth festooned with *bronze
doré*.   *Height, 19 inches*

5. SET OF FOUR BRONZE DORÉ WALL SCONCES   *Louis XVI Style*
Three-light sconce chiseled with cherub groups; fitted for electricity. (*May*)
                                        Height, 16 inches

6. IVORY AND TORTOISE-SHELL TABLE LAMP
Ivory baluster on plinth veneered with tortoise-shell and mounted in *bronze
doré*. Fitted for electricity.   *Height, 29 inches*

7. PAIR DIRECTOIRE BRONZE AND BRONZE DORÉ CANDELABRA FIGURES
Standing classic figures of youth and maiden holding a gilded bronze amphora
with three foliated arms for lights; on round plinth with draped mascarons.
                                        Height, 22½ inches
            [See illustration with number 484]

8. PAIR GEORGIAN LEAD FOUNTAIN STATUETTES
Infant mermen astride dolphins. (*Norden*)   *Height, 14½ inches*

9. SCULPTURED WALNUT PUTTO GROUP
Naked putto carrying another on his shoulders, supporting a shell dish;
signed TOSA.   *Height, 15¼ inches*

9A. BRONZE GROUP   *French, XIX Century*
Winged Victory. In a chariot drawn by two horses.
                            Height, 41 inches; length, 38 inches

9B. BRONZE STATUETTE   *French, XIX Century*
—Abelard. Seated at a writing bench. Signed ANTOCOLSHY, and cast by
Barbédienne, Paris.   *Height, 25 inches; width, 17 inches*

390. THREE DECORATIVE OBJECTS
Bronze doré table lamp, pair carved alabaster Grecian urns. [Lot.]
Heights, 25 and 13 inches

22 ⁵⁶

391. BLACK MARBLE AND BRONZE DORÉ MANTEL CLOCK
Tiffany & Co., New York
Bronze doré drum clock suspended between four columns; on oblong base
with appliqué of Apollo driving his chariot. (May)   Height, 23 inches

12 ⁵ᶻ

392. PAIR BRONZE STATUETTES OF LIONS   After Barye
Well modeled standing figures with huge mane and snarling mouth; on vert
antique marble oval bases.   Length, 23 inches

5 0 -

393. SAXE PORCELAIN AND GILDED BRONZE CANDELABRUM   XIX Century
In the Louis XVI taste, with foliated branches and sconces for ten candles, on
gilded bronze base. Wired for electricity. Chipped.   Height, 31 inches

17 ¹ᶻ

394. THREE TABLE LAMPS
Pair of brass, one Canton stoneware. [Lot.] (Heller)
Heights, 13 and 16 inches

Pam

395. TWO CHINESE BRONZE TEMPLE VASES
Of antique form, with loose ring shoulder handles. (Norden)
Height, 12½ inche

Pam

396. KASHAN POTTERY VASE, FITTED AS LAMP   XVIII Centur
Jar sketched with floral motives in cobalt blue and sepia; rich champlev
enamel mounts studded with cabochons. Fitted for electricity.
Height, 25½ inch

60 -

397. PAIR RED PORPHYRY URNS, MOUNTED IN BRONZE DORÉ Louis XII Styl
Bulbous covered urn mounted with four bronze doré bearded mascaron head
continuing as voluted leaf feet.   Height, 19¾ inch
[See illustration with number 542]

60 -

398. PAIR LOUIS XVI GILDED BRONZE AND CRYSTAL GLASS CANDELABRA
Lyre-form frame embellished with pear-shaped glass lustres and having curve
branches for five lights.   Height, 27 inch

40 -

399. BRONZE STATUETTE   Del Nero, Rome, XIX Centu
Nude figure of a young Roman athlete, captioned: Fiamma ed Azzurr
Signed on circular base. On circular black marble plinth and wood pedest
(Norden)   Height of statuette with plinth, 33 inches; of pedestal, 36 inch

15

2. PAIR OLD CHINESE PAINTINGS ON GLASS
One depicting an Emperor being entertained by actors, the other a mandarin
and attendants on the terrace of a pavilion. Parcel-gilded frame.
Height, 22 inches; length, 30 inches

1. PAIR LOUIS XVI BRONZE AND CRYSTAL GLASS CANDELABRA
With scrolled branches for four candles hung with large pear-shaped crystal
lustres.   *Height, 27 inches*

2. DECORATED PORCELAIN VASE AND COVER   *Imari Style*
Octagonal, with domed cover and Imari decoration.   *Height, 28 inches*

3. TWO TABLE LAMPS
Chinese bronze and *cloisonné* vase lamp; and a *blanc de chine* porcelain vase
lamp; with Ko'ssu tapestry shades. (*Norden*)   *Heights, about 24 inches*

4. PAIR CARVED AND GILDED ALTAR CANDLESTICKS   *Italian, XVIII Century*
With metal pricket top.   *Height, 21 inches*

5. LOUIS XVI CARVED AND GILDED CARTEL
                          John Nyberg, Stockholm, XVIII Century
Of classic urn form carved with drapery swags and clusters of wheat.
                                                      Height, 32 inches

. SET OF FOUR FER DORÉ AND ROCK CRYSTAL LUSTRE WALL SCONCES
                                                  Louis XVI Style
Urn of flowers suspended from a bowknot, with two *bobêches*, and hung with
old lustres.   *Height, 16½ inches*
From Bague, Paris

. SILVER CENTREPIECE AND PAIR CANDLESTICKS   *Italian Renaissance Style*
Octagonal bowl and pair candlesticks with elaborate *ajouré* design of leaf
scrollings, the corners with figures of winged herms and putti riding dolphins.
Substandard. [Lot.]
            Height of candlesticks, 11 inches; diameter of bowl, 14 inches

. CARVED MUTTON-FAT JADE STATUETTE, FITTED AS LAMP
Slender standing figure of a maiden, with a *bronze doré* stem of prunus supporting a silk damask shade. Fitted for electricity. *Height, 29 inches*

. PAIR ITALIAN SILVER CANDELABRA AND PAIR CANDLESTICKS
Directoire herm candelabrum with two curved arms for *bobêches;* and pair
old Nuremberg reeded silver candlesticks with square foot. [Lot.]
                                    Heights, 15½ and 8½ inches

[NUMBERS 410 AND 411]

410. FINE LOUIS XVI FER DORÉ AND ROCK CRYSTAL LUSTRE CHANDELIER
A circle of six *bobêches* supported by three leaf-scrolled arms, all hung
beautiful large rosette and tear lustres of rock crystal; with steeple ter:
surmounting a hanging globe at the foot.

Height, 32½ inches; diameter, 19 i

From Bague, Paris

[See illustration]

. PAIR ROCK CRYSTAL LUSTRE WALL SCONCES   *Italian Baroque*
Composed of a wall urn of sunflowers with two metal candle *bobèches*, hung
with large faceted pear and bead lustres.   *Height, 25 inches*
From Bague, Paris

[See *illustration*]

. PAIR ROCK CRYSTAL LUSTRE WALL SCONCES   *Italian Baroque*
Similar to the preceding.   *Height, 25 inches*
From Bague, Paris

. SIX STAINED AND PAINTED GLASS ARMORIAL PANELS
                                    Flemish, XVII-XVIII Century
Featuring coats of arms and other heraldic motives with legends, composed
of small square panes forming oblong window with wood frame; some imperfect. [Lot.] (*Norden*)
                    Approximate size: Height, 34 inches; width, 22 inches

JAPANESE CLOISONNÉ ENAMEL VASE
Decorated with birds among peony and plum branches in a light blue ground.
                                            Height, 36 inches

. FIVE GLASS AND GILDED METAL WALL LIGHTS
In the early Venetian style, with sconces for three candles.
                                        Height, about 21 inches

. PAIR LOUIS XV TERRA COTTA FIGURES OF CHILDREN
Charming figure of a little girl in laced corsage and summer hat, and another
holding a tambourine, representing Spring. Surmounting square wood plinth.
            Height of statuette, 36 inches; height of pedestal, 24 inches

. PAIR GEORGIAN LEAD GARDEN STATUETTES
Charming figures of scantily draped children representing the seasons of
Spring and Summer, one holding a poke of blossoms, the other squeezing a
bunch of grapes. (*Norden*)   *Height, 32 inches*

. GEORGIAN LEAD FOUNTAIN
Circular *tazza* supported on three juxtaposed swans; in working condition.
(*Norden*)   *Height, 24 inches; diameter, 24 inches*

. LOUIS XV BRONZE DORÉ FIRE SCREEN   *French, XIX Century*
Wire mesh screen, in the form of a rococo cartouche on scroll supports.
                        Height, 29 inches; width, 27 inches

D. LOUIS PHILIPPE CARVED AND GILDED WALL CABINET
                                        French, XLX Century
With glazed front and silk-lined interior. *Height, 29 inches; width, 17 inches*

[NUMBER 422]   [NUMBER 421]

PAIR BRONZE PUTTO GROUPS: NUMBER 376

421. LOUIS XVI INLAID ACAJOU WORK TABLE, MOUNTED IN BRONZE DORÉ
Small oval table with bronze-galleried white marble top, drawer, and tambour shutter; inlaid and banded with light and dark woods.

Height, 31 inches; width, 18 inches

[See illustration]

422. LOUIS XV TULIPWOOD MARQUETERIE OCCASIONAL TABLE
MOUNTED IN BRONZE DORÉ
Small oblong table inlaid in floral lattice design in light woods, the drawer fitted for writing purposes. Bronze-mounted cabriole supports.

Height, 28½ inches; width, 22 inches

[See illustration]

3. BRONZE-MOUNTED AND DECORATED SMALL COMMODE *Louis XVI Style*
Two drawers and undershelf painted with pastoral subjects and flowers.
Brocatelle marble top with pierced bronze gallery.
Height, 35 inches; width, 26 inches

4. LOUIS XVI CARVED AND GILDED GUÉRIDON *French, XIX Century*
Classic tripod with circular top and marble shaped triangular base.
Height, 37 inches

5. DIRECTOIRE ACAJOU DESK CABINET *French, circa 1800*
Pedestal cabinet equipped with five pasteboard filing boxes, leather-lined
hinged slant top. *Height, 47 inches; width, 23 inches*

6. LOUIS XVI CARVED AND CANNÉ WALNUT WINDOW BENCH
French, XVIII Century
Caned ends crested with carved laurel and fruits, caned seat with cushion,
on six tapering round legs. *Length, 5 feet 8 inches*

7. OLIVE WOOD PRIE-DIEU DESK AND BENCH
Prie-Dieu in two parts veneered with strikingly figured light wood, and
carved with griffins; both inlaid with the word *Jerusalem*. [Lot.]
Width of prie-Dieu, 28½ inches

LOUIS PHILIPPE CARVED AND GILDED OCCASIONAL CHAIR
French, XIX Century
Back and seat in antique brocade.

. HUMIDOR CHEST PLAQUÉ WITH OLD DUTCH PICTORIAL TILES
Rectangular chest of metal and wood, the lid and sides covered with a series
of old Delft tiles, each skilfully painted in monochrome with scenes from the
life of Christ and biblical subjects, a few of the tiles imperfect. (*Norden*)
Height, 12 inches; length, 22 inches

NEST OF THREE VENETIAN OCCASIONAL TABLES, AND TRAY
Painted with flowers, and with loose tray top. *Width, 27 inches*

. LOUIS XV INLAID KINGWOOD FALL-FRONT WRITING CABINET
French, XVIII Century
Standing rectangular cabinet, with let-down hinged front revealing pigeonholes and small drawers; two doors below enclosing shelves. Some interior
restoration, and marble top damaged. *Height, 44 inches; width, 25 inches*

. LOUIS XIV CARVED AND GILDED ARMCHAIR IN JARDINIÈRE VELVET
French, XIX Century
High back and seat in colored cut silk jardinière velvet.

433. LOUIS XVI ACAJOU COMMODE, MOUNTED IN BRONZE DORÉ
Three-drawer rectangular commode decorated with gilded bronze moldings;
white marble top with pierced bronze gallery.

95-

Height, 33 inches; length, 43 inches

434. LOUIS XVI CARVED, LAQUÉ, AND CANNÉ LOVE SEAT French, XIX Century
Small *confidante*, the frame painted white and gold. Loose brocade cushion.

10-

Length, 45 inches

435. DIRECTOIRE FRUITWOOD WRITING TABLE   French, Late XVIII Century
Leather-lined oblong top, small drawer in front, tapering round supports.

45-

Height, 26 inches; length, 28 inches

436. LOUIS XVI GRAY LAQUÉ AND BROCADE ARMCHAIR French, XVIII Century
Small *fauteuil*, the back, seat cushion and armpads covered in brocade
arabesque design.

60-

[See illustration]

[NUMBER 437]   [NUMBER 436]

FOUR DIRECTOIRE IVORY LAQUÉ CHAIRS IN APRICOT VELVET
                              French, Late XVIII Century
Armchair and three side chairs with flaring rectangular back, shaped seat and
tapering round supports. Covered in apricot silk velvet.

[See illustration of armchair]

LOUIS PHILIPPE CARVED AND GILDED CONSOLE AND PIER MIRROR
                                  French, XIX Century
Tall oval mirror carved with love birds and flowers, the console similarly
carved, and with composition marble slab. [Lot.]
            Height of console, 36 inches; height of mirror, 5 feet 5 inches

CHINOISERIE DECORATED PAPER THREE-FOLD SCREEN
Depicting a Louis XV motive comprising figures, trees, birds, and pergolas,
after Philippe de la Salle.   *Height, 5 feet 2 inches; length, 5 feet 6 inches*

LOUIS XVI INLAID TULIPWOOD ENCOIGNURE, MOUNTED IN BRONZE DORÉ
Small segmental corner cabinet with door, inlaid and banded with light and
dark woods, and enriched with gilded bronze mounts. Gray St. Anne marble
top.   *Height, 35 inches; width, 17½ inches*

PAIR CARVED FRUITWOOD BERGÈRES OF THE RESTAURATION
                              Southern French, Early XIX Century
In the Egyptian taste, with intricately carved splat and caned seat. Rose
velvet loose cushion.

LOUIS XVI CARVED AND GILDED WINDOW SEAT AND BANQUETTE
                                  French, XIX Century
One in flowered brocade, the other with crimson damask loose cushion.
                                  Length, about 35 inches

LOUIS XVI INLAID TULIPWOOD COMMODE   *French, XVIII Century*
Small shaped rectangular cabinet of two drawers, on tapering curved supports.
Bronze mounts and figured white marble top.
                                  Height, 33 inches; length, 32 inches

REGENCE CARVED WALNUT DAYBED
Shaped head panel, carved stiles, and tapering curved supports. With box
spring, mattress, and bolster.   *Length, 6 feet 6 inches; width, 30 inches*

LOUIS XV INLAID BOIS DE ROSE POUDREUSE   *French, XVIII Century*
Oblong top with three hinged flaps uncovering compartments, one fitted with
mirror; two drawers and slide in front, tapering curved supports.
                                  Height, 30 inches; width, 29 inches

[NUMBER 446]

446. LOUIS XVI BEAUVAIS TAPESTRY FIRE SCREEN

Consisting of an arched rectangular panel of silk tapestry finely woven with a bouquet of blossoms and leaves in delicate colors against a light celadon background. Carved and gilded frame. *Height. 50 inches; width. 33 inches.*

From Duveen Bros., New York

[See illustration]

447. ROSEWOOD MARQUETERIE VITRINE CABINET, MOUNTED IN BRONZE DORÉ

French, XIX Century

Mirrored and plush-lined interior, glazed front and sides; elaborate gilt bronze mounts. *Height, 5 feet 8 inches; width, 36 inches.*

448. LOUIS XVI INLAID KINGWOOD BOUILLOTTE TABLE MOUNTED IN BRONZE DORÉ

Circular table with bronze-galleried white marble top, two slides and drawers in the frieze, tapering square supports with bronze shoes.

Height, 30 inches; diameter, 23 inches.

LOUIS XVI CARVED AND GILDED WALL MIRROR   *Italian, XVIII Century*
Frame pierced and carved with openwork rocaille scrolls and foliage.
Height, 41 inches; width, 29 inches

PAIR LOUIS XVI CARVED, GILDED, AND CANNÉ LARGE BERGÈRES
French, XIX Century
High rectangular back, seat, and arms filled with cane; seat cushion and armpads in crimson damask; also two pillows.

FIVE LOUIS XVI CARVED, GILDED, AND CANNÉ OCCASIONAL CHAIRS
French, XIX Century
Three have shaped back and seat, two square back and seat, filled with cane.

LOUIS XVI FRUITWOOD MARQUETERIE POUDREUSE
Piedmontese, XVIII Century
Hinged rising top lined with green baize and mounted with mirror, damask-lined fitted frame; three drawers in the front. Inlaid with light woods.
Height, 30 inches; width, 30 inches

TWO CRYSTAL GLASS LUSTRE CHANDELIERS IN THE GEORGIAN TASTE
Entirely composed of glass on wire frame. (*Norden*)   *Diameter, 14 inches*

THREE CRYSTAL GLASS LUSTRE CHANDELIERS IN THE GEORGIAN TASTE
Similar to the preceding. (*Norden*)   *Diameters, 11 and 14 inches*

PAIR LOUIS XVI CARVED AND GILDED FAUTEUILS IN RED VELVET
French, Late XVIII Century
Oval back and rounded seat covered in old red silk velvet, the gilded frame carved with beading, leafage, and husk swags.

GLASS AND SILVERED METAL HALL LAMP IN THE GEORGIAN TASTE
Hanging lantern on shaft bound in red cord. (*Norden*)   *Length, 54 inches*

PAIR BRONZE MOUNTED ACAJOU WHAT-NOTS   *Louis XVI Style*
Three bronze-galleried kidney-shaped shelves and white marble top.
Height, 29 inches; width, 16 inches

PAIR LOUIS XV INLAID SYCAMORE PETITES COMMODES
Italian, XVIII Century
Small shaped commode with two drawers, tapering curved supports, and Siena marble top. With restorations, and one marble slab damaged.
Height, 33½ inches; width, 21 inches

[NUMBERS 374 AND 459]

459. LOUIS XV INLAID KINGWOOD SMALL COMMODE, MOUNTED IN
BRONZE DORÉ   French, XVIII C
Small *bombé* commode in the style of Roussel with three drawers and
returns. Elaborate foliated *bronze doré* handles and mounts. *Rouge*
marble top.   Height, 34 inches; width, 31
[See illustration]

110 -

460. LOUIS XVI CARVED, GILDED, AND CANNÉ LOVE SEAT
                                               French, XIX C
With red velours cushion.
                                               Length, 44

Pun

461. LOUIS XVI ACAJOU BOOK CABINET, MOUNTED IN BRONZE DORÉ
                                               French, XIX C
In the style of Riesener, with two metal grilled doors enclosing shelve
veined white marble top (damaged).   Height, 51 inches; width, 43

70 -

[NUMBERS 379 AND 462]

2. RÉGENCE FRUITWOOD READING TABLE WITH
   NEEDLEPOINT SCREEN PANEL   *French, XVIII Century*
   Of charming simplicity, with leather-lined hinged tablet on strut, two drawers, tapering curved supports, and at the back a rising panel lined with
   contemporary *pavot* needlepoint.   *Height, 39 inches; width, 34 inches*
                         [See illustration]

3. LOUIS XVI BROCADE-LINED CARVED AND GILDED FOUR-FOLD SCREEN
                                               French, XIX Century
   Panels lined with ivory silk brocade, mounted with old French mezzotint
   engravings.   *Height, 5 feet; width, 56 inches*

4. RÉGENCE CARVED BEECHWOOD AND CANNÉ FAUTEUIL DE BUREAU
                                               French, XVIII Century
   Back and seat cushion in crimson velours; voluted and carved frame with
   restorations.

[NUMBER 465]

465. PAIR LOUIS XV AUBUSSON TAPESTRY AND CARVED
FRUITWOOD ARMCHAIRS   French, XVIII C
Commodious chair, the shaped back, seat, and armpads covered in tape
the period woven with suspended baskets of flowers and bouquets in
ground. Partly restored frame carved with groups of flowers and leav

[See illustration]

466. VERNIS MARTIN DECORATED ACAJOU VITRINE   French, XIX C
With mirrored interior, glazed front and sides, and glass shelves.
bronze rocaille mounts.   Height, 5 feet 11 inches; width, 27

LOUIS XV CARVED AND GILDED PIER MIRROR

Southern French, XVIII Century

Rectangular frame carved with leaf guilloche and beading, openwork cresting of acanthus scrolled flowers and amatory emblems.

Height, 54 inches; width, 34 inches

LOUIS XVI BRONZE-GALLERIED ACAJOU TABLE   French, *XVIII Century*

Oblong top of white marble bordered with pierced bronze gallery, molded drawer in front, a pull-out slide at either end, on tapering round supports.

Height, 29 inches; length, 32 inches

LOUIS XV CARVED WALNUT AND DAMASK SIDE CHAIR

French, XVIII Century

Provincial chair with framed back and seat in red damask.

LOUIS XVI LAQUÉ AND GILDED PIER TABLE

Southern French or Italian, XVIII Century

Ivory *laqué* segmental top, the frieze, tapering supports, and shaped stretchers richly carved with entwined ribbon and flower ornament, leafage, and fluting.

Height, 34 inches; length, 59 inches

LOUIS XV CARVED WALNUT AND BROCADE SIDE CHAIR

French, XVIII Century

Carved cabriolet frame, the back and seat in antique yellow silk brocade.

PAIR DIRECTOIRE LAQUÉ CONSOLES

Segmented top on spirally turned supports, *laqué* slate green and gold.

Height, 30 inches; width, 25 inches

TALL ACAJOU FILING CABINET OF THE RESTAURATION

French, Early XIX Century

Tall narrow cabinet, equipped with eleven pasteboard filing boxes simulating tooled leather.

Height, 6 feet 8 inches; width, 22 inches

CARVED WALNUT AND CANNÉ DAYBED   *Louis XVI Style*

Caned ends and back. Furnished with box spring, mattress, and five cushions in crimson satin damask.

Length, 7 feet; width, 38 inches

LOUIS XVI GILDED BRONZE AND CRYSTAL GLASS CHANDELIER

Openwork bronze frame elaborately ornamented with glass pendant lustres and rosettes, and with curved arms for eight electric lights.

Diameter, 29 inches

[NUMBER 476]

476. IMPORTANT SET OF FIVE PAINTED CANVAS MURAL PANELS
               School of Philibert-Louis Debucourt, French, circa 18
Mediterranean scenes, showing figures of gentlefolk and peasants anim
harbor and river views, also Roman and medieval ruins. Fine drawing
coloring.

Dimensions of three panels: Height, 84 inches; width, 65 in
Dimensions of two panels: Height, 84 inches; width, 33 in

[See illustration of one]

300-

6A. DECORATED LEATHER THREE-FOLD SCREEN
Decorated with panels of fruits in the Spanish taste.
Height, 5 feet 10 inches; width, 5 feet

77. INLAID AND CARVED MAHOGANY LONG-CASE CLOCK
Hendrik van Voorst, Dutch, XVIII Century
Tall case inlaid and carved and with bronze mounts; richly ornamented and
engraved dial shows phases of the moon, days and months. Striking movement.
Height, 8 feet 2 inches

78. DECORATED WALNUT LONG-CASE CLOCK   *Dutch, XVIII Century*
Tall case of walnut veneer inlaid with marquetry and ornamented with three
carved and gilded allegorical figures. Elaborately decorated dial inscribed
Johan Grantham, London. Plays airs on fourteen bells.
Height, 9 feet 4 inches

79. LOUIS XV IVORY AND GOLD LAQUÉ TRUMEAU WITH PAINTING
French, XVIII Century
Overmantel embellishment enriched with *rocaille* gilded moldings framing
mirror glass and painted canvas pastoral composition.
Height, 5 feet 2 inches; width, 49 inches
Note: Recorded on the back of the frame is the following: "*Peint par
Jollin en 1785, dégradé par les prussiens, 1870; réstauré par Madlle. Barbier
en 1872.*"

80. ROSEWOOD MARQUETERIE CHESS AND BACKGAMMON TABLE
MOUNTED IN BRONZE DORÉ   *Louis XV Style*
Hinged top lined in green baize, the frame fitted with a sliding drawer bear-
ing chess and backgammon board. Richly inlaid with panels of flowers on a
ground of light and dark kingwood, and mounted in *bronze doré.*
Height, 30 inches; length, 32 inches

81. LOUIS XV CARVED AND GILDED CONSOLE   *French, XVIII Century*
Frieze and *rocaille* scroll supports elaborately pierced and carved and converging at the base to an *ajouré* shelf. Top covered with slab of *brêche d'Aleppo*
marble.   *Height, 34 inches; width, 26 inches*

[NUMBER 482]

482. SET OF FOUR QUEEN ANNE WALNUT MARQUETRY FIDDLE-BACK
SIDE CHAIRS   *Dutch, Early XVIII Cent*
Violin-shaped open back with carved shell crest, shaped seat, and car
cabriole front legs ending in club feet; back and seat frame richly inlaid w
urns and sprays of flowers and birds, in tinted marquetry. (*Norden*)

[See illustration of two]

483. PAIR QUEEN ANNE WALNUT MARQUETRY FIDDLE-BACK SIDE CHAIRS
                                               Dutch, Early XVIII Cent
Of nearly similar design to the preceding chairs, but larger, and having cl
and-ball feet. Seats similarly covered. (*Norden*)

[Numbers 387 and 484]

4. Louis XV Tulipwood and Kingwood Marqueterie Writing Table
Mounted in Bronze Doré   French, XVIII Century
Gently serpentine oblong top inlaid with an architectural vignette festooned
with blossoms and leaves in light wood marqueterie on a ground of kingwood
bordered with tulipwood framed in a molding of bronze doré. The tapering
and curved supports enriched with fine bronze doré rocaille mounts; a drawer
at one end.   Height, 28 inches; length, 32 inches

[See illustration]

PAINTINGS, DRAWINGS, AND ETCHINGS

485. ORIGINAL ETCHING   *By Seymour Haden*
Kensington Gardens. Harrington No. 12. Published State. Proof, signed ir
pencil. Very fine impression. Gilt frame.

4/0 —

486. TWO EARLY COPPER-PLATE VUES D'OPTIQUE   *Paris, circa 175(*
View of Venice and Florence. Quaintly hand-colored. Framed.

2 0 —

487. ORIGINAL WATERCOLOR DRAWING   *Thomas Rowlandson, British: 1756-182*
An Englishman in Paris. A splendid example of the work of the grea
English caricaturist. Antique gilt frame.
Height, 14½ inches; width, 21 inche

4/5 —

488. EVENING LANDSCAPE   *Leonard Ochtman, American: 185ª*
Village buildings in the hazy light of a setting sun. Signed, and dated 190:
Height, 16 inches; length, 22 inch

/0 —

488A. SPORTING SCENE   *British School, XIX Centur*
A huntsman in pink coat upon a sorrel mount, taking a fence from the lei
(*Ketterlinus*)   *Height, 10 inches; length, 14 inch*

2 0 —

488B. H.I.M. QUEEN MARIA THERESA   *Austrian School, XVIII Centu*
Waist-length portrait in tight gray satin bodice and rose red cloak, wearir
the star of an Order. (*Ketterlinus*)   *Height, 8 inches; width, 6¾ inch*

/0

488C. TWO SPORTING SCENES   *Henry Alken, British: op. 1801-18*
Scenes from a fox hunt, in one a huntsman upon a bay taking a fence fro
the left, the other with figures riding to the right, a man in a pink co
crossing the foreground. Signed. (*Ketterlinus*)
Panel: Height, 10 inches; length, 14½ inch

/0 0 —

489. SUMMER IDYLL   *Gustav Wiegand, N.A., American: 18;*
A placid stream with fishermen in a boat moored by a wooded bank with ha
concealed cottages in the distance. Signed. *Height, 18 inches; width, 15 inc*

4/0 —

Two Watercolor Drawings
Young girls, one with a child, before English cottages and garden flowers. In
one playing with a kitten, in the other watching a fowl. Initialed F. B.
(*Ketterlinus*) *Height, 8¾ inches; width, 6¾ inches*

Stable Interior *W. J. Boogaard. Dutch: XIX Centuhy*
Two horses feeding at a manger of hay, while a young peasant girl enters a
doorway from the right, carrying a pail. Signed. (*Ketterlinus*)
Panel: Height, 10¾ inches; length, 15¾ inches

View of Rone *John Vanderlyn. American: 1775-1852*
Depicting an old monk looking over the stone wall of an elevated terrace at
a sunlit view of the city of Rome. Signed. (*Ketterlinus*)
Height, 16 inches; length, 24 inches

Still Life
Apples, vegetables and culinary utensils grouped on a table. Signed. G.
Martiny. *Height, 21 inches; length, 25½ inches*

Landscape with Figure *R. Gourdan, French XIX Century*
A clump of gnarled trees on a wild heath, a peasant woman in the foreground.
Signed. *Height, 24 inches; width, 18 inches*

A Sibyl *Attributed to Guido Reni, Italian: 1575-1642*
Bust-length figure of a young girl with eyes cast upwards, her head swathed
in a white turban; brown background. (*Ketterlinus*)
Height, 24 inches; width, 20 inches

. Diana *Noel Coypel, French: 1628-1707*
Reclining beneath a canopy is the goddess with her attendants, watching her
followers hunting bear, stag, and boar. (*Ketterlinus*)
Height, 26½ inches; length, 37 inches

493. WEST POINT ON THE *HUDSON*, 1859

David Johnson, N.A., American: 1827-19

35 — Verdant foreground framed by trees, with a solitary figure in a red shawl looking towards the winding river and mountainous farther shore. Signed with monogram, and dated 1859.   *Height, 22¼ inches; length, 30¼ inches*

494. PORTRAIT OF A GENTLEMAN

Attributed to Daniel Mytens the Younger, Dutch: 1644-16

5 0 — Bust-length of a man in a red doublet and jerkin and large brown turban turned to half-right and holding a miniature in his left hand.

Cradled Panel: Height, 24 inches; width, 19 inches

494A. S. FELIX AND S. MARK: TWO PAINTINGS

Atelier of Peter Paul Rubens, Flemish: 1577-16

7 0 — Head-and-shoulders portraits of the bearded saints in brown cloaks, S. Felix facing to the right; dark backgrounds. (*Ketterlinus*)

Height, 19 inches; width, 14¾ inches
Height, 20¼ inches; width, 16½ inches

Note: The *S. Felix* is said to be a study for the portrait of Rubens' *Confessor*, the model for *S. Felix* in the large picture now in the Versailles Gallery, and formerly in the collection of W. G. Coesvelt, London.

495. NUDE   *L. Balgley, French: Contemporary*

5 — Three-quarter seated figure of a young girl, a white robe drawn over her back. Signed. (*May*)   *Height, 36 inches; width, 23½ inches*

496. PORTRAIT OF A GENTLEMAN   *American School, XVIII Century*

Pass — Bust-length figure of a man facing the observer, in brown coat and white periwig.   *Height, 26¼ inches; width, 20¼ inches*

496A. PORTRAIT OF A LADY   *Rembrandt Peale, N.A., American: 1778-18*

Pass — Portraying an elderly woman at waist length to half-right seated in a crimson armchair; she wears a transparent frilled cap and fichu over a black dress. (*Ketterlinus*)   *Height, 30 inches; width, 25 inches*

497. LANDSCAPE WITH ANIMALS AND FIGURES

Jan Breughel and Johann Rottenhammer: Flemish, XVII Century

37 — A clearing in the forest, with the goddess Diana and attendant nymphs resting after the chase; hounds, trophies, and flowering anemones occupy the fore ground.   *Height, 38 inches; length, 40 inches*

498. LANDSCAPE WITH FIGURES   *German School, XVII Century*

15 — A wooded clearing on the banks of a river, where are seen the goddess Diana with attendant nymphs, an obelisk on the left.

Height, 32 inches; length, 47 inches

). VIEW IN THE SWISS ALPS   *G. Battista, Italian: XIX-XX Century*
Mountain torrent between fir-clothed banks, a snowy peak in the distance.
Signed.   *Watercolor: Height, 43 inches; width, 34 inches*

). SPRINGTIME   *M. Mathieu-Lolliot: French, XIX Century*
Portrait of a lady in summer costume, her pinafore filled with blossoms.
Signed, and dated 1899.   *Height, 45 inches; width, 32 inches*
Exhibited at Paris Salon

. LANDSCAPES AND FIGURES: TWO PAINTINGS   *Follower of Poussin*
Depicting winding streams flowing through broad valleys, before mountainous backgrounds, the views framed by towering trees and peopled with figures.
          Height, 37 inches; length, 52½ inches

. LANDSCAPES AND FIGURES: TWO PAINTINGS   *Follower of Poussin*
Similar views. Companions to the preceding.

. VIEW OF VESUVIUS FROM SORRENTO *G. Battista, Italian: XIX-XX Century*
Mount Vesuvius viewed across a stretch of bay from a rocky promontory.
Signed.   *Height, 51 inches; width, 36 inches*

.. LADY OF THE LILIES   Frederic Stuart Church, American: 1842-1923
Three-quarter length of a young woman in diaphanous green frock, standing
among lilies. Signed, and dated 1905.   *Height, 34 inches; width, 23 inches*

. PORTRAIT OF A MAN
Bearded Semitic in red cap and brown cloak. Artist unknown.
          Height, 27½ inches; width, 22 inches

TAPESTRIES

. THREE AUBUSSON TAPESTRY CHAIR COVERS
Each woven with a basket of flowers or fruit, upon a green mound, in a *tête
de nègre* ground. [Lot.]

. FLEMISH TAPESTRY PANEL   *XVII Century*
Depicting a wooded landscape with a view of an extensive town, with figures
of a man and woman in the foreground.
          Height, 3 feet 5 inches; length, 4 feet 1 inch

. FLEMISH VERDURE TAPESTRY PANEL   *XVIII Century*
Depicting a meadow with view of a church, enclosed by a curtain of foliage,
with a pheasant perched in the foreground. Repaired.
          Height, 4 feet 8 inches; length, 6 feet 2 inches

509. FLEMISH VERDURE TAPESTRY PANEL   XVIII Century
Landscape with tall trees, in which can be seen a pheasant, and partly con-
cealing a view of farmhouses; floral border. Assembled piece.
Height, 6 feet 10 inches; width, 3 feet 6 inches

510. AUBUSSON TAPESTRY   Gothic Style
Depicting a group of noble youths and ladies in a meadow gathered around
a table upon which is a virginal, one of the youths with a falcon on his wrist
a maiden holding a sheet of music; tête de nègre border of white blossoms and
brown and purple grapes.   *Height, 7 feet 10 inches; width, 5 feet 11 inches*

511. AUBUSSON CHINOISERIE TAPESTRY
Tête de nègre field, woven with curious green islands bearing quaint figures
of Chinese in prayer, playing horn and triangle, walking through fantastic
landscapes, and otherwise engaged, the central group depicting an official
carried in a palanquin by four servants with feathered headdresses; floral
border.   -   *Height, 5 feet 10 inches; length, 7 feet 2 inches*

512. AUBUSSON PERGOLA TAPESTRY   Renaissance Style
Woven with a gilded urn filled with blossoms, upon a tessellated terrace with
twisted caryatid columns supporting an arcade adorned with fruit and flowers
in the distance, a vista of an Italian garden. Particolored brown and mauve
border, with russet acanthus leafage and stems of flowers.
Height, 8 feet 5 inches; width, 5 feet 4 inches

[See illustration]

513. FLEMISH RENAISSANCE HUNTING TAPESTRY   Late XVI Century
Depicting numerous mounted and dismounted figures hunting the stag and
boar in a forest with a *château* in the distance; in the foreground, Orphe
charming the wild animals with his lyre. Border filled with allegorical figures
and clusters of fruit and foliage; lower border missing.
Height, 9 feet; length, 13 feet 6 inch

514. AUBUSSON MILLEFLEURS TAPESTRY   Gothic St.
Depicting the figure of a maiden in armor, with sword and baton, beneath
banderole with Gothic inscription; in a dark blue field woven with a beauti-
millefleurs design of clusters of roses, marguerites, cornflowers, lilies-of-t'
valley, and other flowers, with figures of two hares flanking an escutche
below.   *Height, 7 feet 5 inches; width, 5 feet 6 inc*

[NUMBER 512]

515. LOUIS XIV AUBUSSON TAPESTRY   Late *XVII Century*
THE COURT OF DIDO. The figure of the Queen in green robes and rose beige
cloak is seated beneath the canopy at the left, before a cluster of marble
columns; two handmaidens are in attendance upon her, and two others are
carrying a golden vessel through the glade at the right to deposit it with the
heap of golden treasure at her feet. Particolored *tête de nègre* and yellow
border, with clusters of flowers and fruit and green foliage entwined with
spirals of ribbon.   *Height, 9 feet; length, 10 feet 1 inch*

200_

[See *illustration*]

516. LOUIS XIV AUBUSSON TAPESTRY   Late *XVII Century*
BELLEROPHON AND THE CHIMERA. Depicting the crowned bearded figure of
Amisodarus in a formal park beneath an apple tree, attended by the winged
chimera strutting on the grass near an ornamental fountain; in the sky above
appears the armored figure of Bellerophon, riding upon the winged white
horse Pegasus. *Tête de nègre* border with clusters of flowers, fruit, and grapes
in shades of blues, grays and tans, yellows and green. The border is an
assembled one.   *Height, 9 feet 5 inches; width, 6 feet 11 inches*

275

ORIENTAL AND AUBUSSON RUGS

517. TWO RUGS
Small Afghan prayer rug with Nomadic design; Mosul rug with rows of
'pear' motive in blue field. (*Norden*)

20-

518. KASHAN RUG
Woven with a tangle of blossoms in a rose field with sapphire blue pendent
lotus medallion; brick red border with a 'vine' of lotus.
          Length, 6 feet 7 inches; width, 4 feet 2 inches

100-

519. KASHAN MILLEFLEURS RUG
Ruby field woven with a Joshaghan leaf trellis enclosing green weeping
willows, and jewel-like jasmine and lotus blossoms; sapphire blue border
leaf plaquettes.   *Length, 6 feet 9 inches; width, 4 feet 10 inches*

25

520. SAROUK RUG
Scarlet field with a pendented midnight blue and rose lotus medallion;
de nègre floral rosette border. *Length, 6 feet 4 inches; width, 3 feet 10 inches*

70-

521. KASHAN MILLEFLEURS RUG
Scrolled sapphire blue field with sky blue pendented medallion, overrun by
a profusion of lotus, jasmine, and peonies with scrolling creepers, with
sapphire blue lotus border.   *Length, 6 feet 7 inches; width, 4 feet 5 inches*

20-

[NUMBER 515]

522. KAZAK RUG

Lapis blue field woven with three ivory, crimson and green latchhooked octagonal medallions, within three ivory floral borders.

Length, 7 feet 3 inches; width, 5 fee

3 ſ

523. ANATOLIAN SILK 'TREE OF LIFE' RUG

Ruby ground occupied by an elaborate flowering 'Tree of Life' framed in border of cyprus motives and vines on blue.

Length, 9 feet; width, 6 feet 4 inch

4 ſ

524. TEHERAN HERATI CARPET

Sapphire blue field woven with a minute Herati trellis of rosettes and curled leafage; crimson border of floral plaquettes and leafage.

Length, 11 feet 3 inches; width, 7 feet 6 inch.

110 -

525. SERAPI CARPET

Field of bright red and ivory white occupied by a pole medallion of strong conventionalized leaves and flowers on deep blue; the wide border match the central medallion.

Length, 12 feet 9 inches; width, 9 feet 4 inch

180 -

526. MESHED KIRMAN CARPET

Scalloped tawny rose field, centring a cusped stellate medallion in blue a ivory, and overrun with curving branches of flowers; deep blue and ivo floral borders.

Length, 14 feet; width, 7 feet 5 inch

100 -

527. SAROUK CARPET

Double-arched field of *vieux rose*, centring a crimson and sapphire bl diamond medallion, the whole overrun with a straggling *millefleurs* design soft colors; ruby red border of green leaf plaquettes joined by angular flo branches.

Length, 17 feet 10 inches; width, 12 f

2 v ſ

528. PERSIAN HERATI CARPET

Midnight blue field woven with the symmetrical Herati rosette trellis w curving blue leafage; within narrow blue and yellow floral borders.

Length, 12 feet 9 inches; width, 9 feet 9 inc

100 -

529. BIJUR KURD RUG

Serrated hexagonal ruby field with midnight blue pendented floral diam medallion and spandrels; ruby floral border with mazarine blue guards.

Length, 12 feet 3 inches; width, 8 feet 1 i

80 -

530. LOUIS PHILIPPE AUBUSSON CARPET   French, *XIX Cen*

Field occupied by an elaborate *rocaille* cartouche of scrolls and flowers a Duplessis, in shades of maroon, soft yellow, tan, scarlet, green, and wh in a light field.

Length, 18 feet 10 inches; width, 16

175 -

[See illustration of part]

531. LOUIS PHILIPPE AUBUSSON CARPET   *French, XIX Century*
Featuring a circular floral medallion framed within a running border of leaf
rinceaux and garlands of roses in delicate pastel pinks, blues, and soft tans
in a white field, bordered with a running band of patera ornament on rose
pink ground.   *Length, 17 feet 3 inches; width, 13 feet*
From Duveen Bros., New York

532. AUBUSSON CARPET
Wine red cartouche-form field, with a greenish gray medallion and spandrels
ornamented with gilded leaf scrollings and floral nosegays, within a floral
border.   *Length, 16 feet; width, 12 feet 6 inches*

FRENCH AND ITALIAN FURNITURE (CONCLUDED)

533. FOUR RÉGENCE CARVED BEECHWOOD AND CANNÉ CHAIRS
Two armchairs and two side chairs, with caned backs and seats; loose cushions
in rose brocade; cabriole legs and curved stretchers.

534. LOUIS XV INLAID ROSEWOOD WRITING TABLE
MOUNTED IN BRONZE DORÉ   *French, XIX Century*
Shaped oblong top lined with dark leather showing cracks and tears; three
drawers at one side, and elaborate bronze mounts.
                                     Height, 30 inches; length, 56 inches

535. LOUIS XVI INLAID ROSEWOOD AND TULIPWOOD COMMODE
                                     Piedmontese, Late XVIII Century
Rectangular chest of three long drawers richly inlaid and banded with various
woods; on tapering square legs.   *Height, 41 inches; length, 49 inches*

536. LOUIS XVI INLAID WALNUT AND SYCAMORE COMMODE
                                     Piedmontese, Late XVIII Century
Variation of the preceding, with three drawers and carved supports.
                                     Height, 38 inches; length, 47 inches

537. LOUIS XVI CARVED AND GILDED SETTEE IN AUBUSSON SILK TAPESTRY
Long rectangular back, seat, and armpads covered in Aubusson silk tapestry,
woven with urns of flowers and leaf *rinceaux*, in delicate pastel colors in an
ivory ground. Frame carved and gilded.   *Length, 5 feet 2 inches*
From Duveen Bros., New York

                    [See illustration]

[NUMBER 537]

PAIR LOUIS XVI CARVED AND GILDED ARMCHAIRS IN AUBUSSON
SILK TAPESTRY
En suite with the preceding settee.
From Duveen Bros., New York

PAIR LOUIS XVI CARVED AND GILDED SIDE CHAIRS IN AUBUSSON
SILK TAPESTRY
En suite with the preceding.
From Duveen Bros., New York

LOUIS XVI WHITE AND GOLD LAQUÉ BANQUETTE French, *XVIII* Century
On six cabriole legs; top in worn brocade.   *Length, 46 inches*

VERNIS MARTIN VITRINE TABLE   *Louis XV Style*
Interior lined with silk velvet; gilded bronze mounts.
                    Height, 29 inches; width, 21 inches

[NUMBERS 397 AND 542]

542. RÉGENCE INLAID PALISSANDRE COMMODE MOUNTED IN BRONZE DORÉ
French, XVIII Century

Bombé commode with three drawers and white veined rose marble top.
Drawers, returns, and supports ornamented with elaborate gilded bronze
rocaille scroll and foliage mounts. *Height, 34 inches; length, 50 inches.*

[See illustration]

543. EIGHT-FOLD COROMANDEL LACQUER SCREEN
Ch'ien-lung

Depicting a procession of figures before an Emperor seated in a pavilion with
warrior attendants, on the seashore, the upper and lower panels occupied by
Flowers of the Seasons and 'antique' objects. Needs a few repairs.

Height, 6 feet 10 inches; length, 9 feet 4 inches.

[See illustration]

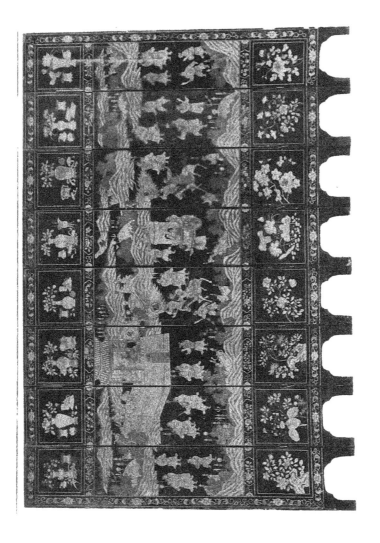

544. ACAJOU BEDROOM SUITE, MOUNTED IN BRONZE DORÉ   *Louis XV Style*

A pair of bedsteads with chased head and foot panels, box spring, and mattress; four-drawer commode surmounted by swivel mirror; a chiffonier with five drawers and two doors; night stand, writing table with one drawer, *2 5 0 —* bergère and two occasional chairs covered in striped silk, and a canopy. Cabinet pieces with brocatelle marble tops. Also pale blue *moiré* bed coverlets, canopy, draperies, two bolsters, and two pairs of window hangings with valances *en suite;* lined and interlined with sateen. [Lot.]

Width of bedstead, 50 inches; length of commode, 42 inches; height of chiffonier, 5 feet

Collection of Julian Le Roy White and others. American Art Association. 1924

545. BRONZE-MOUNTED ACAJOU VITRINE CABINET   *Louis XVI Style*

40 — With mirrored and velvet-lined interior, and decorated panels.

Height, 5 feet; width, 31 inches

546. LOUIS XVI WHITE AND GOLD PAINTED PIER MIRROR

French, XVIII Century

45 — Tall rectangular panel with carved and gilded moldings framing two panels of mirror glass, the crest embellished with a group of amatory emblems.

Height, 6 feet 3 inches; width, 25 inches

547. STEINWAY GRAND PIANO

Case of satiny textured mahogany, with tapering square supports. Serial *380 —* Number 129267.

Width of keyboard, 56 inches

548. DECORATED AND PARCEL-GILDED CABINET ON STAND   *Louis XII Style*

With shelves enclosed by two doors, painted with pastoral figures; elaborately *30* carved and parcel-gilded supports.

Height, 5 feet; width, 39 inches

549. CARVED WALNUT AND CANNÉ SETTEE   *Régence Style*

Caned voluted back and arms, richly carved skirt and short scrolled legs; loose *40 —* cushion and five loose cushions in flowered brocade.

Length, 6 feet

550. BRONZE-MOUNTED ACAJOU VITRINE CABINET   *Louis XV Style*

With mirrored and velvet-lined interior and galleried top.

Height, 53 inches; width, 29 inches

17.12 551. LOUIS XVI CARVED AND GILDED MARQUISE IN SILK LAMPAS

French, XIX Century

20 — With rounded back, valanced skirt, tapering short legs. Covered in silver and blue silk lampas.

Length, 43 inches

552. ELABORATELY CARVED AND GILDED WALL MIRROR

German, XVIII Century

35 — Rectangular frame and shaped high openwork crest elaborately pierced and carved with *putti*, flowers, and foliage.

Height, 6 feet 2 inches; width, 37 inches

. LOUIS XV CARVED AND GILDED SALON TABLE   French, XIX Century
With inset white marble top, curved supports and stretchers.
Height, 30 inches; length, 38 inches

. DECORATED THREE-FOLD LEATHER SCREEN   *Louis XV Style*
Painted with medallions of rococo figures on an old ivory ground.
Height, 6 feet; width, 5 feet

A. CARVED OAK TABLE   *Italian Renaissance Style*
Rectangular top on carved leonine end supports.
Height, 33 inches; length, 5 feet 4 inches

. VERNIS MARTIN DECORATED VITRINE
In the rococo taste. With glazed front and sides with cabriole supports.
Height, 7 feet; width, 38 inches

. LOUIS XV BRONZE-MOUNTED KINGWOOD WRITING TABLE
French, XIX Century
Shaped oblong top lined with tooled leather, three drawers at one side, elaborate bronze mounts.   *Height, 30 inches; length, 57 inches*

. TWO LOUIS XVI CARVED AND GILDED MARBLE TOPPED TABLES
French, XIX Century
One circular, one triangular, with figured marble tops. One cracked.
Width, about 20 inches

. GILT-FRAMED PIER MIRROR IN THE GEORGIAN TASTE
Rectangular, with narrow frame of gilded gesso. (Norden)
Height, 5 feet 3 inches; width, 44 inches

). GILT-FRAMED PIER MIRROR IN THE GEORGIAN TASTE
Large rectangular mirror with gilded gesso frame. (Norden)
Height, 6 feet 2 inches; width, 51 inches

). GILT-FRAMED PIER MIRROR IN THE GEORGIAN TASTE
Large arched rectangular mirror with gilded gesso frame. (Norden)
Height, 8 feet 4 inches; width, 57 inches

!. PAIR GILDED BRONZE AND STEEL ANDIRONS AND FIRE TOOLS
XVII Century Style
Of baroque design, with elaborate scroll base. Also four fire tools on standard.
Height of andirons, 26 inches

2. PAIR WROUGHT IRON AND BRONZE ANDIRONS   *German Renaissance Style*
Elaborate spiral shaft capped with bronze griffin and mascaron grotesque finial.   *Height, 43 inches*

3. DORÉ ILLUSTRATIONS. Die *Heilige* Schrift Alten und Neuen Testaments.
Illustrated by Gustave Doré. 2 vols., folio, full leather, stamped in blind and gilt, gilt edges; worn, one back loose.   Stuttgart, n.d.

[END OF SALE]

Appraisals

FOR UNITED STATES AND STATE TAX
INSURANCE AND OTHER PURPOSES

❖

Catalogues

OF PRIVATE COLLECTIONS

❖

APPRAISALS. The American Art Association-Anderson Galleries, Ic., will furnish appraisals, made by experts under its direct supervision, of art and literary property, jewelry, and all personal effects, i the settlement of estates, for inheritance tax, insurance, and other purposes.

Upon request the Galleries will furnish the names of many trust ad insurance companies, executors, administrators, trustees, attorrys, and private individuals for whom the Galleries has made appaisals which not only have been entirely satisfactory to them, but have been accepted by the United States Estate Tax Bureau, the State Tax Commission, and others in interest.

CATALOGUES. The Galleries is prepared to supplement this appraisal work by making catalogues of private libraries, of the contents of homes or of entire estates, such catalogues to be modeled after the intelligently compiled and finely printed sales catalogues of the Galleries.

❖

AMERICAN ART ASSOCIATION
ANDERSON GALLERIES · INC

30 East 57th Street, New York City

Telephone: PLAZA 3-1269

Composition and Presswork
by
WB
PUBLISHERS PRINTING COMPANY
William Bradford Press
NEW YORK

Lightning Source UK Ltd.
Milton Keynes UK
UKHW010953061118
331795UK00007B/341/P